CLOTHING Optional

# CLOTHING
## Optional

### And Other Ways to Read These Stories

## ALAN ZWEIBEL

Published in the United States by Villard Books,
an imprint of The Random House Publishing Group,
a division of Random House, Inc., New York.

VILLARD and "V" CIRCLED Design are registered
trademarks of Random House, Inc.

Some of the essays in this work were originally published in
*AARP Bulletin, Atlantic Monthly, Esquire, Los Angeles Magazine,
Los Angeles Times Sunday Magazine, On Writing,*
and *The New York Times.*

LIBRARY OF CONGRESS CATALOGING-IN-PUBLICATION DATA
Zweibel, Alan.
Clothing optional: and other ways to read these stories / Alan Zweibel.
p.  cm.
ISBN 978-0-345-50086-1
1. Zweibel, Alan.  2. Television writers—United States—Biography.
3. Television producers and directors—United States—Biography.  I. Title.
PN1992.4.Z84A3 2008
818'.5402—dc22    2008023242

Printed in the United States of America on acid-free paper

www.villard.com

2 4 6 8 9 7 5 3 1

FIRST EDITION

*Illustrations by Alan Zweibel*
*Book design by Dana Leigh Blanchette*

*For Robin, Lindsay,*
*Sari, Adam, and Cori*

## AUTHOR'S NOTE

Many of the things in this book actually happened. Some of them didn't. When real people's names appear, most of those real people weren't there, someone else probably was. Except, of course, in those instances when the actual people actually *were* there. Understand?

Pearl Blankman

## FOREWORD

*I am a seventy-eight-year-old woman who has witnessed quite a few miracles during my stay on this planet. Phenomena that defied all odds and exceeded all realistic expectations at the time they took place. But finding a cure for polio, putting a man on the moon, and the fall of Communist Russia were simply run-of-the-mill incidences when compared with the most jaw-dropping occurrence of all—that Alan Zweibel, a veritable illiterate when he was a student in my high school English class, became a professional writer. In fact, after reading the following pages, I am convinced the achievement lends proof to the adage that if you give a chimpanzee a typewriter along with an infinite amount of paper and time, it will eventually write a collection of short pieces entitled* Clothing Optional.

*Astonishingly enough, these stories held my interest. Some even amused me. I'm at a point in my life where I can use a good laugh. My husband passed away in April, so I tend to seek out anything that will bring a smile to my face and help me forget my Gerald's waning months,* when the new kidney proved to be as faulty as the one it replaced. So when I found myself giggling while reading "Comic Dialogue," "I Saw Your Mother's Ass," and "Letters from an Annoying Man," I actually forgot they were written by an older version of the same kid whose parents were told that his best chance of getting through four years of college was if he went to a two-year college twice. Likewise, when I read the more poignant entries, like "Notes from a Western State" and "Happy," as well as Alan's moving tribute to his friend and mentor Herb Sargent, I had to remind myself that the only previous time I'd witnessed even a semblance of sensitivity was when he didn't pull both wings off of a fly at the senior picnic.

"Do people change?" I've asked myself. Perhaps. We've all heard that as a student Einstein failed math and then went on to become, well, Einstein. Similarly, Alan Zweibel failed English and then went on to become, well, Alan Zweibel—a writer of modest renown who managed to break two of his toes when he dropped the Distinguished Alumnus Award our school gave him a few years ago on his foot.

Still, I'm impressed with Alan's accomplishments. They serve to reinforce my faith in the capabilities of the human spirit—how a person can combine a great deal of determination with just a modicum of talent and end up being one of the greatest overachievers of his generation. It restores my belief in God and convinces me that it's just a matter of time until the meek inherit the Earth.

Mrs. Pearl Blankman
Hewlett, New York

# CONTENTS

CLOTHING Optional

# My First Love

When the editors of this fine publication asked me to write a Valentine's Day piece recalling the glory of my first love, I found the assignment to be both nostalgic and harrowing, given the many competing loves that emerged at approximately the same time in my then young life. So, after much soul searching, the best I could do was narrow my list of loves down to two choices—my ardent passion for women and my equally fervent feelings for the Old Testament—and combine the two in this heartwarming story titled "The Day I Got Caught Playing with Myself in Hebrew School . . . While Thinking About Abraham's Wife Sarah."

*OCTOBER 1962.* Johnny Carson became the new host of *The Tonight Show.* John Steinbeck won the Nobel Prize in Literature. The Cuban missile crisis brought us to the brink of nuclear war with the Soviet Union. And I was an eleven-year-old Hebrew-

school student at Temple Beth Shalom on the South Shore of
Long Island.

Three afternoons a week I was carpooled to this house of
worship ostensibly to learn about the history of my people. My
teacher was an elderly Old World gentleman named Rabbi
Nathan Levitats, who spoke English pretty much the same way
that I spoke Chinese . . . miserably. Still, he taught us Bible stories, and because the Hebrew name for Alan is Avraham, which
is also the Hebrew name for Abraham, I immediately felt a special kinship with that Old Testament figure known as "the First
Jew" because of his belief that there was only one God.

> *Genesis 14:22* "And Avraham said, 'I lift up mine hand
> unto the LORD, the God of all Gods, the possessor of
> Heaven and Earth.'"

But little did I know, oh, how could I possibly have known,
that Abraham and I would also share a similar taste in women?
That I, too, would fall for Sarah. The beautiful . . .

> *Genesis 15:14* "Behold, Sarah art a fair woman to look
> upon."

. . . yet barren . . .

> *Genesis 15:16* "Sarah was barren."

. . . wife of the first Jew. A woman whose very name, on this particular October day, caused this particular Hebrew-school student to have a missile crisis of his own.

Now, up until this point, my schoolboy crushes were exclu-
sively of the secular kind, which included but were not limited to

female classmates, teachers, the school nurse, the librarian, the lady in the attendance office who gave us passes when we were tardy, the lady with the moustache who sat on that wooden stool behind the cash register in the lunchroom, the vice principal, a crossing guard, and three women on the school board.

And yes, there were two other women. Two other visions of feminine pulchritude whose beauty and grace caused this Hebrew-school boy to stand up, sit down, and make his skullcap spin like a revved-up dreidel. One was Dale Evans, the wife of the very popular cowboy Roy Rogers. The other was Jacqueline Kennedy, the wife of the incredibly handsome thirty-fifth president of the United States. The eleven-year-old Avraham Zweibel loved them both. But there were problems. Dale was married to a western hero who could shoot me while riding on a horse named Trigger. And Jackie was married to the most powerful man on the face of the Earth, who, with just one phone call, could have J. Edgar Hoover dress me up as a woman and have his way with me behind the Jefferson Memorial. Besides, neither of them was Jewish—a detail that would've killed my immigrant grandparents faster than you can say "Yussel, zip up my dress, put on your hat, let's go downstairs, take the #2 bus, transfer at Flatbush Avenue, get off at Brighton Beach, maybe have a bite to eat, then walk to the water's edge and drown ourselves in the Atlantic Ocean."

Enter Sarah. The beautiful, barren wife of the first Jew. She was perfect. Not only was she of our tribe, but according to Rabbi Levitats she was wise and understanding, and the eleven-year-old Avraham Zweibel admired those traits in a woman. Plus, at this point in time, Sarah's husband had been dead for more than three thousand years—so really, who would I be hurting?

And so what if she was barren? I was only eleven and I knew that fathering a child before I finished sixth grade would be problematic considering all the homework I usually had. So this was perfect— What's that, Rabbi Levitats? What are you saying?

*Genesis 17:15* "And God said unto Avraham, 'As for thy wife Sarah, I will bless her and she shall bear you a son and thou shalt call his name Isaac . . .'"

Oh, so she wasn't barren after all. The Almighty himself actually got an assist on that play, which I think was very nice of

him—although it probably didn't take that much effort. My guess is that anyone who took only seven days to create everything that existed would be able to kick-start that ghost town of a uterus without breaking a sweat. Good thing I found out now, though. Sure, I'd *marry* Sarah. Given the opportunity, what red-blooded Hebrew-school student wouldn't have jumped at the prospect of achieving Old Testament immortality by marrying into such a family and forever being referred to as the first Jew-in-law? But as far as fathering her next child— What's that, Rabbi Levitats?

> *Genesis 17:16* "And Avraham covered his face and fell upon his knee and asked the Lord how a child could be born to a man who was one hundred years old and to a wife who was ninety."

Okay. So Sarah was ninety. And I was eleven. Fine. So I'd learn to live without some things. I'd always thought that solid food and direct sunlight were overrated anyway. The important thing was that I loved this woman, so I just sat there thinking and thinking about this withered object of my Hebrew-school-boy affections when—

> *Genesis 22:2* "And the Lord said unto Avraham, 'Take now thy son, thine only son Isaac, whom thou lovest, and get thee into the land of Moriah, and offer him there as a sacrifice upon the mountain I tell thee of.' "

Abraham was taking the kid out of town to kill him! Great! What better time than now to make my move on his ancient wife. So the eleven-year-old Avraham Zweibel saw himself setting off on a trip of his own, back to the biblical town of

Canaan, where I came upon a small hut, knocked upon its door, and heard the soft voice of my Sarah say from inside, "Is that you, Avraham?"

"Well, yes and no," I answered. "I am Avraham Zweibel. But feel free to call me Alan," I told her as she opened the door with the spunk of a woman two years her junior.

I entered Sarah's home and was immediately taken by how truly beautiful she was when she pointed to the gift I'd brought for her and asked, "What is that?" And oh, how beautiful she looked when she laughed, when we *both* laughed, when I said, "Something that you are not," as I handed her a spring chicken.

So now that the levity portion of our date was satisfied, I switched gears to show Sarah that, despite my youth, there was also a sensitive, softer side that I had to offer. "Where is thy husband?" I asked.

I could see the tears begin to well up when she said, "He took our son to the base of a mountain where he plans to tie him to a wooden stake and stab him to death with a hunting knife."

"With all due respect," I said, "that doesn't sound like good parenting," before putting my arm around her and drawing her trembling body closer to mine.

"Oh, Avraham Zweibel," she said, still weeping. "How you understand me so."

"That's because I care, Sarah," I answered while fumbling with the knot on her robe.

"But the one thing I do not understand, Avraham Zweibel, is what *this* is."

"It is what we call a zipper, Sarah. Shall I show thee how it works?"

"Oh, yes, Avraham Zweibel. There is so much I can learn from you, Avraham Zweibel. Oh, Avraham Zweibel. Oh, Avraham Zweibel—"

"Avraham Zweibel? Avraham Zweibel?" How odd. Sarah suddenly sounded different. Her voice had somehow just turned manly. Almost like that of an old, astonished, Old World Hebrew-school teacher.

"What are you doing?" asked Rabbi Levitats in a tone similar to the one I suspected Isaac used when he saw his father come at him with that hunting knife. Needless to say, I was terrified.

"I'm not doing anything, Rabbi Levitats," I said, all the while praying that since this was a Reform temple the man would mark this incident on an incredibly liberal curve.

"Well, see to it that you aren't" is all he said before walking back to the front of the room.

What a relief. A modern-day miracle that spared the tumescent Avraham Zweibel from the ultimate humiliation—and taught me to keep my mind from wandering during Hebrew school. Or, at the very least, to limit my wanderings to the exploits of the seven original astronauts.

As for me and Sarah, well, let's just say that our romance was short-lived. I went on to finish my schooling, embark on a career, and start a family, while my beautiful Sarah, an Old Testament creature of habit if there ever was one, opted to remain exactly where she was in the Bible. So our paths didn't cross again until my youngest daughter, Sari, was Bat Mitzvahed. And her haftorah was, I swear, the story about Abraham taking Isaac away to sacrifice him. And throughout the entire service, the Torah readings, and her speech, I was blushing, just a little.

# Can I Have a Million Dollars?

—Can I have a million dollars?

—Excuse me?

—Can I have a million dollars? Why are you making that face?

—That's quite a request.

—Not really.

—How do you figure?

—Look, we've been friends a long time, right?

—Right.

—And you have around four hundred million dollars, right?

—About that, yes.

—So all I'm asking you for is a measly million.

—Is that all?

—I know it sounds like a lot. . . .

—That it does.

—That's because you're not looking at it properly.

—Then how should I be looking at it?

—Well, let's say you had four hundred dollars. Would you give me one?

—Sure.

—Okay, and if you had four thousand dollars. Would you give me ten?

—Probably.

—So? Do the math. It's the same thing.

—Not really.

—Why?

—Because this is a million dollars.

—But it's the same percentage.

—But this is a million dollars. And that's a lot of money to loan someone.

—Oh, I agree.

—You do?

—Yes.

—So?

—So that's why I'm not asking for a loan.

—You're not?

—No. I just want you to give it to me.

—But I don't feel comfortable doing that.

—Fine. Then can you loan me a million dollars?

—Okay.

—Really?

—I can do that.

—Great.

—Any idea when you could pay me back?

—I'm not going to pay you back.

—You're not?

—No. That's a lot of pressure to put on our friendship.

—But . . .

—"Neither a borrower nor a lender be."

—I've heard that saying.

—And it's true. . . .

—I bet.

—That's why it's a saying.

—I guess so. . . .

—Because think about it, if you lend me a million dollars, it's going to be hanging in the air between us.

—Maybe.

—Not maybe, definitely. Whenever we're together you're going to be thinking, "He owes me a million dollars," and I'm going to be thinking, "Shit, I owe him a million dollars."

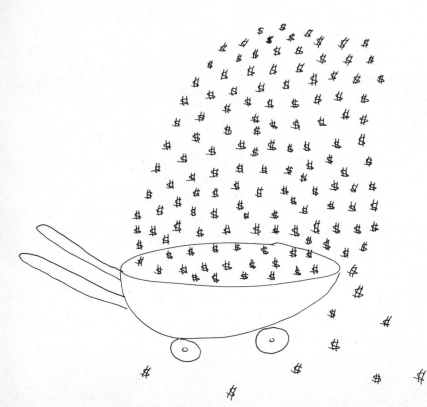

—Perhaps . . .

—And I wouldn't want something like that to come between us.

—Neither would I.

—Your friendship means too much to me.

—Sure . . .

—So that's why you should just give me the million dollars. Clean. With no strings attached. Because God knows it's a lot better than the alternative.

—Which is?

—Me suing you for a million dollars.

—Excuse me?

—And I really don't want that to happen because that would be bad for our friendship.

—I'll say . . .

—Because whenever we're together you're going to be thinking, "He's suing me for a million dollars," and that could lead to hard feelings, and I don't want that.

—Why would you sue me?

—Mental anguish.

—Mental anguish?

—Yeah . . .

—What kind of mental anguish?

—Because it would really bother me if you didn't give me a million dollars.

—Jesus . . .

—I won't be able to sleep, which will affect my moods, and my relationship with family and co-workers.

—And that will be my fault?

—To my mind, yes.

—All because I didn't give you a million dollars.

—To my mind, yes.

—That would be hard to prove, you know.

—I know. A case like that could tie us both up for years. And I would really like to avoid that if at all possible.

—So would I.

—Hey, we both have too much else going on without adding this nonsense to the mix.

—So what are you suggesting?

—That we settle.

—Settle?

—Look, we've been friends a long time. And we're reasonable adults. I'm sure we can come up with a figure that's comfortable for both of us.

—Do you have a number in mind?

—Yep.

—What is it?

—Fifty thousand dollars.

—You want me to give you fifty thousand dollars?

—Look, if you had eight thousand dollars, would you give me one?

—Of course.

—This is the same thing.

—Okay.

—Really?

—I said okay.

—So you'll give me fifty thousand dollars?

—Sure. That all right with you?

—Well, I'm taking a bit of a hit here, but it's worth it.

—For our friendship?

—For our friendship.

# Mrs. Glickman's Deposition

**Setting:**   A lawyer's office in Los Angeles, California.

**Situation:**   Two years ago I was involved in an automobile accident with an eighty-one-year-old woman. Although my insurance company made several attempts to settle with her, she kept insisting that the offers were insultingly low and was now suing me personally.

**Her Claims:**   That, as a result of injuries sustained from the accident, this now eighty-three-year-old woman has not been able to sexually satisfy her now eighty-seven-year-old husband.

**In Attendance:**   Me, the now eighty-three-year-old woman, her now eighty-seven-year-old husband, my attorney, her attorney, and a very fat female court reporter.

*Note: The following are the exchanges, the way I remember them, between my attorney and the now eighty-three-year-old woman, unless otherwise indicated. (I've also changed the old crone's name.)*

Q:  Your name is Rita Glickman?

A:  Yes.

Q:  And you understand, Mrs. Glickman, the oath you just took is the same as if this were a court of law and that the penalty for perjury is also the same?

A:  Yes.

Q:  And you further realize that due to the nature of your claim I may have to get somewhat personal with my questions?

A:  What do you mean?

Q:  Well, in your suit you say that because of the accident with Mr. Zweibel you have not been able to perform your, let's say, marital duties. Am I correct?

A:  Yes.

Q:  This is a legal assertion called "loss of consortion."

A:  Okay.

Q:  So to investigate this fully, I may have to ask some rather embarrassing questions, such as "Before the accident, how often did you and your husband engage in marital relations?"

A:  Four times a week.

Q:  Excuse me?

A: Four times a week.

Q: Perhaps you didn't understand my question—

A: What's not to understand? Before this hooligan slammed into me, Gerry and I had sex four times a week.

Q: And by sex you are referring to . . . ?

A: Intercourse.

Q: Intercourse.

A: Intercourse.

Q: Four times a week.

A: Yes, we had intercourse four times a week. *(The fat court reporter starts blushing.)*

Q: Now, when you say four times a week . . . strike that . . . Was it literally . . . strike that . . . Now, Mrs. Glickman, on the morning of November 18 of last year you had a collision with Mr. Zweibel and you sustained some injuries.

A: Yes.

Q: And what exactly was the nature of those injuries?

A: I had bruises across my chest and contusions in my left hip.

Q: And because of these injuries to your chest and left hip, you claim there was an interruption of yours and Mr. Glickman's regular sexual activity.

A: Yes.

Q: And why was that?

A: I was in too much pain to accommodate the weight of my husband's body . . .

*(Everyone steals a peek at the now eighty-seven-year-old Gerry Glickman.)*

A:      . . . plus, he likes to move around a lot and I just couldn't keep up.

*(Everyone steals another peek at the now eighty-seven-year-old Gerry Glickman.)*

Q:      I see. And for how long were you unable to accommodate your husband's weight and movement . . . strike that . . . How long was it until you and your husband were able to resume normal marital relations?

A:      Seven months.

Q:      So you're saying that following your accident with Mr. Zweibel, for seven months you had—

A:      No sex.

Q:      And after those seven months, when all your wounds were healed, you and your husband returned to your regular rate of intimacy?

A:      Yes.

Q:      Which is . . . ?

A:      Four times a week.

Q:      Four times a week.

A:      Yes.

Q:      *(under his breath)* Four times a week . . .

Her Lawyer:   Counselor . . .

Q:      Okay, okay, Mrs. Glickman, you do know that there are other ways . . . strike that . . . Mrs. Glickman . . . were there any other ways you were able to show affection during this seven-month period?

A:    Other than kissing and hugging?

Q:    Yes.

A:    No.

Q:    You couldn't show affection?

A:    No, I couldn't.

Q:    And why was that?

A:    Because I also hurt my jaw.

Her Lawyer:    Jesus.

My Lawyer:    Oh my.

Me:    God help us all.

Q:    I would like to remind you that you are under oath, Mrs. Glickman.

A:    But I *did* hurt my jaw. It's right there in my hospital records.

Q:    Yeah, yeah, I saw them. . . . Now, were there any other injuries from this accident that affected your marital relations with Mr. Glickman?

A:    Well, I did suffer a loss of hearing.

Q:    Your hearing loss has hurt your sex life?

A:    Yes.

Q:    How so?

A:    Because sometimes it's difficult for me to hear what Gerry would like me to do, and this throws our timing off. You see, Gerry's very expressive, and if I'm looking at him, I can read his lips. But when I'm facing another direction and Gerry issues a command—

Her Lawyer:    I think this would be a good time to take a break.

My Lawyer:     Me too.

      Me:     God help us all.

*During the break, the court reporter made some phone calls, Mrs. Glickman read a magazine, and everyone else followed her now eighty-seven-year-old husband into the men's room.*

## Letters from an Annoying Man

For the most part, writers are not famous. Even the most successful ones fail to turn heads or grace the covers of tabloids unless they happen to marry or do something terrible to somebody who *is* famous. No matter how expansive their body of work or how highly regarded their contribution to the culture, they are an anonymous bunch whose celebrity may, at best, be limited to name recognition or familiarity with something they've written. This is hardly a new phenomenon, as legend has it that even Shakespeare himself had trouble getting laid without a name tag and sixteenth-century photo ID.

Personally, I've come to accept my lot in public life. I learned early on that acknowledgment from strangers would have to come secondhand when my words are spoken by actors. If my words hold interest and receive laughs, the best I can hope for is that people will make a point of remembering who wrote them. And if I happen to be in the back of the theater shouting, "Hey, I wrote those words!" the chances of my being recognized are likely to increase accordingly. Shy of that, people tend to leave me alone. Except, that is, for a man named Kevin Traverson.

*Dear Mr. Zweibel—*
   *I just read your book,* The Other Shulman. *Could you please autograph this copy and send it back to me in the enclosed self-addressed stamped envelope?*
                    *Sincerely yours,*
                    *Kevin Traverson*

*Dear Mr. Traverson—*
   *Thank you so much for your kind words about my book—which I am returning with the autograph you requested. I'm so pleased that you enjoy my work.*
                    *Your pal,*
                    *Alan Zweibel*

*Dear Mr. Zweibel—*
   *While I appreciate your prompt response, I must say that I was terribly disappointed when the copy of your book arrived and I saw the inscription. Sure, I can understand how you'd think that "To Kevin, This book is really good" is a cute thing to write but, quite frankly, I didn't think that your book was really that good. In fact, I thought it was just okay. So I am returning that copy with the hope that you will send me another one that merely has your signature on the title page.*
                    *Thank you,*
                    *Kevin Traverson*

*Dear Mr. Traverson—*

*Sorry that it has taken me so long to get back to you, but I've been on a 31-city book tour promoting my novel (the one you think is just "okay" despite all the great reviews it's been getting) and have fallen behind on my correspondence. Enclosed is a personal copy of my book with a new autograph. I hope it's to your liking.*

*Sincerely,*
*Alan Zweibel*

*Mr. Zweibel—*

*Couldn't help but notice that you signed your last letter "sincerely" as opposed to "your pal." How come? Because I didn't like your book? One would think you'd have a thicker skin by now, as I see that not all critics gave it the raves you referred to. I've enclosed a handful of those less than "great reviews" along with the book you sent me. I'm returning it to you because the copy I sent you was a first edition; the one you sent back was a second printing. Was this an oversight? Or a subtle way of telling me that your novel has actually sold enough copies to have a second printing despite what I think of it as well as the picture of you on the inside cover? I saw you on TV and couldn't help but notice that you've either aged dramatically since your book came out (are you sick?) or your publisher decided to print a picture of a young man who looks like he could eventually look like you.*

*Kevin Traverson*

Kevin—

   Enclosed please find an autographed copy of a first
edition of my book. Funny thing—I almost sent you a
signed copy from the third printing. It's a good thing I
double-checked!!!!

                    Alan Zweibel


Mr. Zweibel—

   I received the copy of your signed first edition and was
relieved to see that you finally got it right.

   And I guess congratulations are in order—I just read
that The Other Shulman was nominated for the Thurber
Prize for American Humor. I'm speechless. One can only
conclude that this has been a slow year for the comic novel.

   But I'm proud to say that I'm letting your good news
inspire me. A few years ago I started writing my own novel
but had to put it aside when my aging mother took sick.
Eventually, she stopped aging and died. It was hard at first

but I now feel ready to resume writing, and that's where
you come in. Enclosed are the first 247 pages of my book.
I think it's real good (I'm about a third of the way through
the story) but really need a pair of fresh eyes to read it,
give me detailed notes, and help me figure out how the
remaining twenty-three chapters should go.

  Thank you very much.

                    Sincerely,
                    Kevin


P.S. When you go through my manuscript, please pay
particular attention to the character named Van Cliburn.
I thought it was a great name since he works for a
moving company (get it? Van? Moving van?) but I'm now
wondering if people would get confused with the real Van
Cliburn, who's a pianist. Do you think they will? Should
I change the character's name? Or do you think it's okay
because everyone knows that the real Van Cliburn is 73
years old and would never work for a moving company?


Dear Mr. Traverson—
  Thank you for your kind words about the Thurber
nomination. I consider it quite an honor to be in the
company of the other nominees—all of whom are widely
considered to be among the greatest comic minds of this
generation.

  And thank you for your confidence in thinking that I can
be of help with your novel. As a fellow writer, I know how
precious our material is to us and how much trust we must
have to show it to someone while it's still a work-in-progress.
So I'm flattered that you have such faith in me.

However, I'm afraid that I must decline. At the moment I am incredibly overwhelmed with my own workload and I don't think it would be respectful to you or your material if it's relegated to a back burner where I won't be able to get to it for a few months, at the very least.

Again, I appreciate your thoughts and wish you the best of luck with your book, which I am returning unread.

> Sincerely,
> Alan Z.

Dear Big Shot—

So you have no time for me, huh? Have so much work of your own that you can't read the first 247 pages of my novel, do you? Well, then how do you explain that piece you wrote for Sunday's NY Times Op-Ed page? Where you said that when you ran the New York City Marathon, at the starting line you purposely stayed toward the back of the pack of 33,000 runners "for pretty much the same reason that cowboys, if given the choice, would prefer to be behind the horses during a stampede."

Sound familiar? No? Well, it should. I'm referring to page 64 of the manuscript you claim to not have read. Where I say, "When Van Cliburn was a young boy, before he decided to become a professional mover, he wanted to be a wrangler even after his father told him all about stampedes."

Still say you haven't read my novel? Or, in the very least, the third paragraph on page 64? I find that hard to believe. Almost as hard to believe that someone of your supposed stature would stoop so low as to steal from me.

I demand an explanation.

> Kevin Traverson

*Dear Thief—*
   Still *waiting for an explanation.*

                    *An Impatient Kevin Traverson*


*Hey Shithead—*
   *My attorney's name is Elliott Throneberry. Don't say I didn't warn you.*

                    *You Know Who*


*Dear Mr. Throneberry—*
   *I am in receipt of your registered letter and, given the letterhead on your stationery, can only assume that you are indeed a lawyer. And it's a rather generous assumption at that, given the caliber of client you appear to be representing.*
   *That being said, allow me to set the record straight with the sincere hope that this matter continues no further. One: I did not read your Mr. Traverson's manuscript. Two: To the best of my knowledge, Mr. Traverson does not own the word* stampede. *It is in the dictionary, and last I looked, his name was nowhere to be seen near its listing. However, on the off chance that I am mistaken and that word* stampede *is indeed his, and his alone, to use; may I suggest you forget about me and give serious thought to suing John Wayne's estate, as they have a lot more money than I do and he used the word more than anyone I can think of?*
   *Sorry to cut this letter short, but I just heard an ambulance drive by and I suspect you have to get ready to go chase it.*

                    *Shysterly yours,*
                    *Alan Zweibel*

*Dear Mr. Zweibel—*

*Congratulations on your book winning the Thurber Prize for American Humor!!!! It is so richly deserved and has already been a boon to me as I sold the copy you sent me on eBay for a price that should go even higher with the holiday season quickly coming upon us. Toward that end, can you please autograph these twelve copies and send them back in the enclosed carton? My attorney says it's the least you can do given all the stress I've suffered at your hands, and I tend to agree. I feel it can serve as an excellent first step in the healing process.*

*Your Biggest Fan,*
*Kevin Traverson*

*Dear Kevin—*

*Enclosed please find the copies of my novel that you sent me. And while I did not sign them as you requested, please note that I did enclose a jar of petroleum jelly, which should no doubt make it that much easier for you and your attorney to take turns shoving all twelve books up each other's ass. And though I don't know it firsthand, I can only presume that it will also help in your healing process.*

*Your pal,*
*Alan Zweibel*

# Clothing Optional

Let me just say at the outset that as I write these words, I am fully clothed. Shirt. Pants. Shoes. You know the look. Now, this is a point writers rarely feel the need to make. Traditionally, they simply go about the task of setting down words with little or no mention as to which parts of their anatomy are covered or exposed. I envy those writers. I used to be one of them. Allow me to explain.

About a month ago, the pressures of script deadlines made the task of arranging dialogue between characters running around on a movie screen an all-consuming one—to the extent that any distraction was deemed so intrusive, I was absolutely livid when pulled out of a rehearsal to take a call from this magazine.

"Alan, would you ever give any thought to spending time at a nudist club and writing about it?"

"Yes."

"You can go there whenever you—"

"Yes."

"And you can write the piece whenever you—"

"Yes."

"Any idea when you might be able—"

"Now."

"I mean, you're extremely busy, so—"

"Now."

"But all of your other projects—"

"They can wait. How much do I owe you?"

"For . . . ?"

"Letting me do this."


## A CALL TO MY WIFE

"Hello?"

"Hey, Robin! Guess what? I've been asked to write about a nudist club in Palm Springs."

"I'm not going."

"Who invited you?"

Reaction from the rest of my family ranged from my son, Adam, fourteen, begging me to take him along, to my youngest daughter, Sari, seven, who giggled at the thought of "Daddy seeing lots of tushies," to my embarrassed middle daughter, Lindsay, eleven, who—as I left in the third inning of her West L.A. softball game—found it easier to tell her teammates I was going to the hospital for minor back surgery.

There were other reactions as well. The most asked question: Are you going to get naked? The least asked: Where are you going to insert your room key when playing naked volleyball? (My dad lost sleep over this one.) The person with the most questions: me. And I started asking them as I turned onto I-10 heading east toward the desert: Why am I doing this? Did I bring enough sunblock? Why am I doing this? When was the last time I was naked in front of a nude woman whom I wasn't married to and with whom I shared a hamper and three children? What if I run into someone I know? Like Siskel? Or Ebert? Or one of my mother's friends? What if I get an erection? What if I get an erection in front of one of my mother's friends? Why am I doing this? And why in God's name am I sweating this much?

The air-conditioning in the car was on full blast, yet as I got closer and closer to the exit that would lead me to the land of naked people, my pores were involuntarily soaking every stitch of fabric associated with my forty-four-year-old body, and I was now sort of hoping that somewhere between my daughter's softball field and all of those windmill things, I'd contracted malaria and would have to call my editor with my regrets and suggest she send a non-Jewish male to research this article.

The place I was driving toward? The Terra Cotta Inn, which according to the brochure was a "clothing optional" resort. So with the distinct possibility that it was nerves and not a rare tropical disease that was causing me to sweat like a fountain, I began to hang on to the word *optional* the way that actress in *Cliffhanger* hung on to Sylvester Stallone's hand.

## THE TERRA COTTA INN

I can't remember ever knocking more gently than I did on the big gray doors that separate the Terra Cotta Inn from the traffic on East Racquet Club Road. But after a few seconds, the door opened. A woman, dressed only in a romper unzipped to her navel, greeted me. Standing beside her was a completely naked man.

"Alan?"

"Yes."

"I'm Mary Clare."

"Hello."

"And this is my husband, Tom."

"Hi, Alan."

"Nice to meet your penis, Tom."

Rendered mute by their unique brand of desert hospitality, I obediently followed Mary Clare and Tom around a half wall, which gave way to a courtyard. With a pool. Bordered on three sides by attached rooms. And swimming in the pool, lying on the grass near the pool, reading books and Sunday papers on lounge chairs that surrounded the pool, and walking around, casually sipping drinks nowhere near the pool, were them—the naked people. Two-eyed, four-cheeked naked people, who obviously didn't know the meaning of the word *optional*.

My hosts couldn't have been nicer. They explained that this was strictly a couples resort, where people come with their significant unclothed others to enjoy the sun and relax. The last thing they want is for anyone to feel pressured into walking around in any way that would make them uncomfortable.

But as much as I appreciated the inherent logic of this policy, anyone who has ever been the only sober person at a party knows how it's possible to feel like the only one who's drunk under those circumstances. I, for one, had never felt goofier than when I was unloading the car.

The fact that I brought luggage to a nudist resort is, in itself, worthy of some discussion. But how I felt carrying three suitcases and a hanging garment bag through a maze of lounging naked people on the way to my room on the far side of the pool is a topic Talmudic rabbis could debate for centuries. Suffice it to say that Robin had done my packing, and it took me close to forty-five minutes to determine what I was actually going to wear to a naked tea. My decision? Gym shorts and a Yankees nightshirt that extended just below the knee. My thinking? Hard to say. But for some reason, it felt just right.

## THE NAKED TEA

The office of the Terra Cotta Inn is not dissimilar to the office of any typical resort that happens to have thirty-six stark-naked adults and one large Jewish man in a Yankees nightshirt having wine and hors d'oeuvres on a Sunday afternoon. Husbands. And wives. Girlfriends. And boyfriends. Youngish. And oldish. Blackish. And whitish. Chitchatting about the weather. The Dodgers. Clinton. And Dole. Conspicuous by its absence was any overt acknowledgment of one another's overabundance of exposed flesh. They were all so natural. And casual.

Could I possibly be like that? So cool? So nonchalant? I went outside to where everyone had drifted back to their previous locations in and around the pool. I took off my gym shorts. No big deal—courtesy of my Yankees nightshirt—but a start. And then? Oh, what the hell. Off came the nightshirt, and into the pool I dove. Butt naked. Like the day I was born, only larger and more immature.

Under the water I swam. Eyes open, mindful of any exposed body parts that might be dangling in my path. At the other side of the pool, I came up for air, and right before me was a rather plump, elderly couple sitting on the edge, minding their own business. I turned around, took a deep breath, and headed underwater back to the other end, where I surfaced only to find myself, God help me, looking into, God help me, the nether regions of a beautiful woman sitting with her legs, God help me,

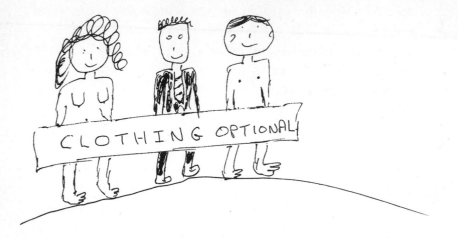

apart. And then . . . well . . . it happened. The *e* word. Right there, in the pool. Well, let's just say I had no choice but to swim back (now with the aid of a rudder) toward that plump, elderly couple whose very presence, God bless them . . . humbled me.

## A CALL HOME

"Are you naked right now, Daddy?"
"No, Sari. Can I please speak to Mommy?"
"Okay."
"Thanks, honey."
"Hey, Dad, you take any pictures of the naked folks?"
"No, Adam. Can I please speak to Mommy?"
"Okay."
"Thanks, kiddo."
"Dad?"
"Hi, Lindsay."
"Dad, when you come home, could you limp in front of my

friends? The way you would if you actually had minor back surgery?"

"Fine. Can I please speak to Mommy?"

"Okay."

"Thanks, sweetheart."

"Hello?"

"Robin?"

"Yeah?"

"Could you drive out here?"

"When?"

"Now."

"Now?"

"Please?"

"Why?"

"Because I'm hornier than a toad."

"Alan, the kids have school tomorrow."

"Robin, I was around naked people all day, and now it's night, and I'm alone, and I'm ready to burst."

"Alan—"

"Please. It's only a two-hour drive. You can come out, stay seven minutes, then turn around and go home."

"You gotta be kidding."

"You're right. Six minutes."

I hung up, got undressed, went outside, and was aware of the fact I had never done those things in exactly that order before.

The Terra Cotta Inn doesn't have a restaurant. (If it did, I wondered, would the chef have to wear two hairnets?) But meals ordered in arrive in no time at all, as the delivery boys from all the local restaurants race through the streets so they can get to see the home where the naked people roam.

I heard voices and walked in their direction. Much to my surprise, I now had no inhibitions about my nudity. Sure, I was conscious of it, but there I was. Under the stars. Four couples. And me. At a naked pizza party. A couple from L.A. whose children knew where they'd gone for the weekend but weren't told about the clothes part; a middle-aged CEO from Michigan and his wife of twenty-seven years; a kindergarten teacher and her husband, a retired cop, who've been coming to places like this since 1987; a couple from San Diego, both attorneys and both thirty-two, and me.

I realized I liked these naked people. They were without pretense in addition to being without clothing. So the next morning, when I saw a number of them pass my window holding coffee mugs and doughnuts, I took off my bathrobe and dashed outside to join them. Not only did I spend the entire morning naked, but by noon, I found the very concept of clothing an absurd one.

## A CALL TO A FRIEND

"Garry, it's Alan. Look, I'm calling because I just felt the need to tell someone that I'm forty-four years old, and about an hour ago, for the first time in my life, I put suntan lotion on my ass. I'll explain later. Bye."

What else can I say other than that I was now one of them? I swam naked. I read *American Pastoral* by Philip Roth naked. I ate a chef's salad naked. I played naked foosball. I started using my laptop for reasons other than to just cover my lap. And I was quickly becoming more and more intoxicated with my newfound freedom.

"Hi, Tom."

"Hi, Alan. Where you headed?"

"Carl's Jr. The one on Palm Canyon. Want anything?"

"No, thanks."

"Catch you later, Tom."

"Alan?"

"Yeah?"

"Do you think you should put some pants on?"

"What for?"

"Well, the Palm Springs police have rules when it comes to naked men and fast-food chains."

"What about the drive-thru?"

"Also the drive-thru."

"Those bastards."


## ANOTHER CALL HOME

"Well, then how about taking a plane?"

"Alan . . ."

"I'm serious, Robin. The airport's only a few miles from here, and—"

"But you're coming home tomorrow."

"Exactly. So I say fly out in the morning, I'll pick you up, bring you here, then we'll drive back to L.A. together."

"We'll see."

"Really?"

"Yeah, yeah."

"Great, because I really want you to see this place and meet my new friends."

"Jesus . . ."

"Hey, guess what? Remember when I told you that years ago, this place was where President Kennedy and Marilyn Monroe used to come together?"

"Yeah . . . ?"

"Well, local legend has it they used to stay in room thirty-four, and I went in there today."

"Yeah . . . ?"

"Naked."

"Yeah . . . ?"

"So think about it, Robin. This very afternoon, I was naked in the same exact room that a president and Marilyn Monroe were naked in."

"Yeah . . . ?"

"So the way I see it, in some strange, mystical way, this afternoon I had sex with Marilyn Monroe and . . ."

"Here, speak to the kids."

"What kids?"

## GOING HOME

Since I had a 114-mile trip ahead of me, I planned on leaving Palm Springs no later than eleven in the morning. This would allow me more than enough time to stop off at the Nike outlet store on the way, maybe grab a little lunch, and still make Lindsay's softball game, which began at three. This was a very workable, very well-intentioned plan, but . . .

I've seen a lot of prison movies where inmates, when their terms are up, are so comfortable with the routine that they prefer to remain in jail for fear they won't be able to adjust to life on the outside. And while this is by and large a feeling they have after fifty years in Alcatraz or Shawshank, I felt exactly the same way after two days at a clothing-optional resort. And since I had no idea when I'd have the opportunity to be naked outside again, I savored my last few garmentless hours, and before I knew it, it was noon. No big deal. Nike won't go broke without my business. So I took another naked swim, finished Philip Roth's book, noticed that a very attractive woman was checking in, started reading *To Kill a Mockingbird* (because I hadn't read it since eighth grade), and the next thing I knew, it was almost one o'clock. Oh well, I've always felt lunch was an overrated meal. And I still had two solid hours to travel the 114 miles, so all I'd have to do is maintain a 65-mph pace, and I'd get to the field for the start of Lindsay's game. I packed, got dressed, said good-bye to Tom and Mary Clare, noticed that the very attractive woman who'd just checked in was now emerging from her room completely naked, put down my luggage, read a few more pages of *To Kill a Mockingbird,* marveled at how much I'd forgotten about this fine piece of writing, and, when I finally pulled out of the parking lot at two o'clock, wondered aloud how it would actually feel to drive a car 114 mph.

Would I ever go back? I think so. With my wife? God knows. But those questions would have to wait.

When I pulled up to the softball field, it was the fourth inning. And as I approached the bleachers, I purposely limped the way one would if he'd actually had minor back surgery.

## My NYC Marathon

Today, I am sorry to say, I will not be running in the New York City Marathon because I've been out promoting my novel about a man who is running in the New York City Marathon and I didn't have time to train. I didn't run in last year's marathon either because I was busy writing my novel about a man who is running in the New York City Marathon and I didn't have time to train. I did, however, run in the 2003 New York City Marathon. I trained hard for that one. I joined a running group, did stretching exercises, watched my diet, and finished in 33,517th place. A half hour slower than the time of my previous marathon, for which I didn't train at all.

I harbor not even the slightest embarrassment that while I was running, a person could have gotten a good night's sleep. Or have consecutively boiled 127 three-minute eggs. Or that while I was still hauling my fifty-three-year-old carcass through the streets of Brooklyn, the winner had not only crossed the finish line at Tavern on the Green but was probably already on a plane back to Kenya.

None of those things bother me because my goal was modest. All I wanted was to finish. To allow the cheers of the crowds to carry me through the five boroughs and allow me to revisit some neighborhoods I hadn't seen since childhood. In effect, a tour. I knew my limitations and had no illusions that by dint of a good night's sleep I would miraculously get a burst of energy and become the new winged symbol for FTD.

So at the start of the race, I lined up toward the back of the pack for pretty much the same reason that cowboys, if given the choice, would prefer to be behind the horses during a stampede. And after the gun sounded, it was thrilling being a part of a 35,000-strong throng moving en masse across the Verrazano-Narrows Bridge on a beautiful November morning. I also appreciated the wit displayed by my fellow marathoners who had shunned the traditional running shorts and T-shirts and were

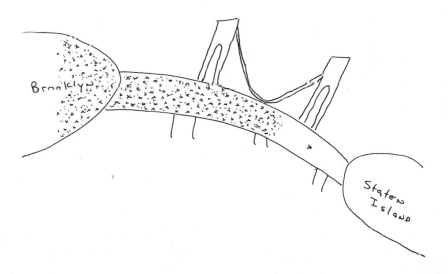

dressed, oh, let's call it unconventionally, for the 26.2-mile journey. Among them were a bride, a man wrapped in an American flag bouncing red, white, and blue basketballs, a one-legged waiter carrying a bar tray with a mug of beer attached to it, Abraham Lincoln, a surgeon, and what I believe was a deli clerk. It supplied added color to an already colorful event, and I didn't even mind when they all passed me—figuring that they either were better runners than me or might eventually drop out of the race when they felt their joke was over.

The polar bear did bother me, however. A lot. Whether it was a thin person wearing two hundred pounds of white fur or a very fat person wearing a tight furry sweater, I'm not sure, but I first noticed him when he scampered past me in Williamsburg, where he was given high fives by Hasidic families who ignored me when I eventually came upon them. Was it possible that, as they were snubbing me, he turned back in my direction and waved at me before turning around and disappearing into the masses ahead? No, I figured. He was probably waving to an amused child who had called out to him or to another tundra-dwelling mammal who was also running that day. So I proceeded along and figured I had seen the last of him because there was no sighting in all of Queens.

Manhattan was another story. For when I came across the Queensboro Bridge, panting and carb-depleted, I turned up First Avenue and spotted him again. Leaning against one of the refreshment tables that are stationed at every mile marker and eating a bagel. The thought that there were still ten miles to go until the race ended in Central Park was, indeed, a daunting one under normal circumstances. But after a polar bear makes eye contact with you a second time, gestures as if offering you a bite of his sesame bagel, folds his paws onto his chest, and does an Arctic jig before turning around and heading uptown, you can't help but feel stupid. And unathletic. So I grabbed a bagel of my own and took off. For the sake of accuracy, when I say "took off," I mean that I trudged along in the same direction determined to catch up—which I almost did when he waved to me after he drank some Gatorade in the Bronx, after he had stopped to play the harmonica with a street band in Harlem, and after he crossed the finish line about fifty yards ahead of me in Central Park.

To this day it is hard for me to believe that someone dressed as a polar bear actually beat me in the New York City Marathon. Yes, I know I said that just completing the race was victory enough, and it was. Still, once this book tour is over, I plan to start training for next year's marathon with another goal in mind—to finish ahead of anyone dressed similarly, so my children will stop laughing at me.

## Mendel

Then spake Joshua to the Lord in the day when the Lord delivered up the Amorites before the children of Israel and he said "Sun, stand still." . . . And the sun stood still until the children of Israel had avenged themselves upon their enemies.

—JOSHUA 10:12

*EXT. THE OTHER SIDE OF THE WORLD — NIGHT*

*A confused Mendel is pacing in front of a buffet table.*

MENDEL

Why is it still dark? I don't understand it. Granted, I am but a simple caterer. However,

it doesn't take a great scholar to know that
the night should be followed by the morning—and not by another night.

*Mendel looks toward heaven.*

> MENDEL *(cont'd)*
> Where is it? Isn't there someone who can tell
> me where the sun is?

*Mendel starts pacing again.*

> MENDEL *(cont'd)*
> What's the sense of fooling myself? Nobody
> can explain it. How could they possibly ex-
> plain it? Every mortal I know has overslept.
> Oh dear God—while my beautiful spread
> turns rancid, my entire village sleeps.

*Mendel looks toward heaven.*

> MENDEL *(cont'd)*
> Tell me, dear God—what in your name is
> going on?

> GOD
> What's the problem?

> MENDEL
> What's the problem? I thought you were all-
> knowing.

GOD

I am.

MENDEL

So? Can't you see what's wrong?

GOD

Not really. It's sort of dark.

MENDEL

That's the problem.

GOD

Oh.

MENDEL

Well? How come it's still dark?

GOD

Excellent question, Mendel. You're very in-quisitive for a caterer.

MENDEL

Thanks, but . . .

GOD

The fact is, you woke up too early. Go back to sleep.

MENDEL

I . . .

GOD

Maybe I should do the same.

*(bad acting)*

I know I'm the Supreme Being, but trust me,
I too am groggy. Pleasant dreams.

*We hear God yawning. Mendel starts pacing again.*

MENDEL

Woke up too early? How can this be? Last
night was no different from any other night:
I arrived home, said a prayer, washed up,
made a blessing, sat down, begged for for-
giveness, turned around, said I'm sorry, had
my supper, then beat my breast. . . . Afterward, I read the Bible, discussed it at length
with my wise son, was hit across the mouth
with it by my wicked son, then fed it to my
simple son. Then my wife and I sang, we
danced, we cleaned the ram, we said our
prayers, we spun the dreidel, we celebrated
the harvest, we knew each other in a biblical
sense, then we went to bed.

*Mendel looks to heaven.*

MENDEL *(cont'd)*

No, dear God. I got my basic eight hours of
sleep. . . . God? God?

> GOD
> *(feigning weariness)*

Yes, Mendel.

> MENDEL

I figured out that I woke up the same time I usually do.

> GOD
> *(disappointed)*

Oh, you did.

> MENDEL

Yes. And if you'll pardon my skepticism, dear Lord, I can't help but think that you are keeping something from me.

> GOD

Me?

*Mendel nods.*

> GOD *(cont'd)*

Well, if I should tell you the truth, do you promise not to get a swelled head? Because you've been given an honor.

> MENDEL

Me?

> GOD

Yes.

MENDEL

Do tell.

GOD

No, I better not.

MENDEL

I beg of you. I can use a lift.

GOD

Well, the reason it is dark is because there's an eclipse.

MENDEL

A what?

GOD

A culinary eclipse. Once every five hundred years I align the Earth between the sun and a caterer— plunging the planet into temporary darkness. Congratulations.

MENDEL

Wait a second . . .

GOD

But let's keep this between us, okay? You can imagine how hectic my life would get if every caterer started asking for his own eclipse.

MENDEL

You're lying, aren't you?

GOD
A liar? The Almighty you call a liar?

MENDEL
I'm not saying that lying is a prominent trait
of yours.

GOD
But you just . . .

MENDEL
What I meant, dear God, was that in this particular instance I solemnly believe that you
are divinely yanking my proverbial chain. Is
this so?

GOD
I'll be right back.

*EXT. THE OTHER SIDE OF THE WORLD — DAY*

*A very tan Joshua is on the battlefield.*

GOD
Joshua . . . Joshua.

JOSHUA
Who may I say is calling?

GOD
Don't get cute.

JOSHUA

Oh, hi. Some war, huh?

GOD

So you've won?

JOSHUA

Hey, these things take time. But we'll be all
right. Those Amorites are dropping like flies.

GOD

I need the sun.

JOSHUA

When?

GOD

Now.

JOSHUA

Come again?

GOD

Or as soon as possible, anyway.

JOSHUA
*(aside)*

Great guy . . .

GOD

Excuse me?

JOSHUA

Here I am risking my life for you, all I ask for
is one favor, and you . . .


GOD

For me? You're risking your life for me?


JOSHUA

No, for me. . . . Of course it's for you. *I* have
no ax to grind with the Amorites—this is all
for you.


GOD

How do you figure?


JOSHUA

These Amorites are heathens. They spend
most of their time womanizing and getting
drunk . . .


GOD

They do?


JOSHUA

. . . and doing whatever their animal instincts
dictate.


GOD

But don't they fear my wrath?

JOSHUA

Why should they? They don't believe in you
to begin with.


GOD

They don't?


JOSHUA

No.


GOD

God . . .


JOSHUA

What was that?


GOD

Oh, nothing—I was just talking to myself. . . . Look, you believe in me, don't you?


JOSHUA

No, I'm swinging spiked maces out here for
my health. Stop being so insecure.


GOD

Sorry.


JOSHUA

Don't worry about it. Just let me get on with
the war. What's the big rush, anyway?

GOD
Well, this whole sun thing is somewhat of an inconvenience to Mendel . . .

JOSHUA
The caterer?

GOD
Yeah. He's got this smorgasbord and . . .

JOSHUA
Spare me.
*(aside)*
I have an onslaught on my hands and he's talking Jell-O molds.

*EXT. THE OTHER SIDE OF THE WORLD — NIGHT*

*Mendel is fanning the buffet with a small shrub.*

GOD
Mendel.

MENDEL
You smell that? It's the fish.

*God sniffs.*

GOD
Who's this buffet for?

MENDEL

The Brillsteins. In honor of their son's confir-
mation.

GOD

Is that all?

MENDEL

Is that all? Their son is turning thirteen.

GOD

So, I'll make him fourteen. It'll serve the
Brillsteins right for having a surname in this
day and age. Feel better?

MENDEL

No.

GOD

I have an idea. What do you say I pay you for
the smorgasbord? Twelve zuzim. And, I'll
throw in a new tablecloth for your troubles.

MENDEL

No.

GOD

And a jug of wine.

MENDEL

No.

GOD

What're you trying to do, hold me up?

MENDEL

Dear God, I am a simple man, with simple needs. And what meager living I do manage to eke out goes only for the simple comforts of my family—so my faithful wife, Sara, can feel like a lady, and so my simple son, Shlomo, can dress in propeller skullcaps. Is this so much to ask?

GOD

No . . .

MENDEL

So why do you choose to keep me, you should pardon the pun, in the dark?

*Mendel hangs his head in despair.*

*EXT. THE OTHER SIDE OF THE WORLD — DAY*

*The war is still raging.*

GOD

Well?

JOSHUA

Won't be long now.

GOD
Can you give me a ballpark figure?


JOSHUA
What's a ballpark?


GOD
*(trying to keep his composure)*
Ten minutes? Fifteen minutes?


JOSHUA
Don't you have anything else to do? How come you left Moses alone? I didn't see anyone breathing down his neck.


GOD
But . . .


JOSHUA
Don't "but" me. You know you're wrong. You parted the sea for Moses. You gave ten plagues to Moses. You did this for Moses. You did that for Moses.


*Joshua starts jumping up and down.*


JOSHUA *(cont'd)*
Moses! Moses! Moses! Everything went to Moses! Well, I'm sick of it!


GOD
Is it possible that you're overreacting?

JOSHUA

You gave Moses forty years to cross the
Sinai. Forty years! No one told him to hurry
up because of some caterer. But me . . .

*Joshua starts crying.*

## EXT. THE OTHER SIDE OF THE WORLD — NIGHT

*Mendel is pointing a quartz spatula toward his chest.*

GOD

Mendel!

MENDEL

I've got nothing to live for.

## EXT. THE OTHER SIDE OF THE WORLD — DAY

*Joshua is on the ground flailing his arms and legs.*

GOD

Josh . . .

JOSHUA

Leave me alone.

## EXT. HEAVEN — DAY/NIGHT/WHATEVER

*God is pacing.*

GOD

Imagine me, the omnipotent one, with a moral dilemma. Hard to believe. It's mundane, yet harrowing at the same time. On the one hand, we have Joshua, who's fighting a war and risking his mortal existence so that *I* can continue to exist for all those who prostrate themselves in acknowledgment of me as thy Lord, thy God, King of the Universe. While, on the other hand, Mendel isn't even a chef. True, he does cater religious celebrations, but even if his word of mouth is good and his business does flourish, those gluttons will more likely rave about the food than about me. . . . But then again, why should I take this out on Mendel, who wants only to support his loving family? The devout Mendel, who reads the Bible and who believes in me. Or at least he did before all this sun business started—before I let him down.

*(God slaps himself)*

Stop it! This is no time for sentiment. Gotta be practical here. Even a blind man can see that your future's with Joshua. Give him the sun, he'll win the war, and your word will be passed from father to son, generation after generation. While with Mendel . . . who's kidding who? To hell with Mendel.

*(God slaps himself)*

What's wrong with me? Just what kind of deity am I turning into anyway? Didn't I make both Joshua and Mendel in my own image? Do they not both serve me in their own way? Of course they do.

## EXT. THE DARK SIDE OF THE WORLD — NIGHT

*Mendel is perched on the buffet table, readying to hurl his body onto the stone utensils that are pointing upward from the ground.*

> GOD
> Mendel, don't!

> MENDEL
> And tell me why I shouldn't. My business is ruined and the God that I've devoted my spiritual life to has forsaken me. Thanks for nothing.

*Mendel jumps off the table.*

> GOD
> Mendel, stop!

*And, as the Lord speaks, the leaping Mendel freezes, rendering him suspended in midair.*

> MENDEL
> *(looking around)*
> What's this?

GOD

Look, I've been doing some thinking, and I think I've come up with a solution to all of this.

MENDEL

I'm all ears.

GOD

You want to hear it?

MENDEL

I'm suspended in midair. What else have I got to do, plow?

GOD

Okay. Now, I've figured out a compromise. Joshua gets to keep the sun for as long as he needs it . . .

MENDEL

Lovely plan. Please let me fall onto my cutlery.

GOD

. . . and you, you get the real plum.

MENDEL

I can't wait to hear this one.

GOD

Ready?

MENDEL

Yeah, yeah . . .

GOD

Brunch.

MENDEL

What's that?

GOD

A combination of breakfast and lunch.

MENDEL

I never heard of such a thing.

GOD

No one has. But trust me, by the time Brillstein's guests wake up, they'll be dying for it.

MENDEL

Could work.

GOD

It'll be a big hit.

MENDEL

I'll give it a shot.

GOD

Big, big hit.

And it came to pass that Joshua smote the
Amorites and the sun rose upon Mendel's vil-
lage.... And Brillstein's guests devoured the
brunch and said they were stuffed. Whereupon
they returned to their homes, had a snack, said
they were full, had their dinner, said they
couldn't eat another bite, had a snack, and went
to bed.

—ALAN ZWEIBEL

## Herb Sargent

We had just started *Saturday Night Live.* I was an apprentice writer, twenty-four years old, and I felt intimidated. Chevy was hysterically funny. So were John and Danny and Gilda and Franken. And Michael O'Donoghue, well, Michael simply scared the shit out of me. So I stayed pretty much to myself. One day I came to work, and on my desk was a framed cartoon. A drawing—no caption—of a drunken rabbi staggering home late and holding a wine bottle. And waiting for him on the other side of the door was his angry wife, getting ready to hit him with a Torah instead of a rolling pin. I had no idea who'd put it there. I started looking around, and out of the corner of my eye I saw a white-haired man in his office, laughing. He had put it there. That was the first communication I had with Herb Sargent— which was significant, given that he never spoke and he gave me a cartoon that had no caption.

I had seen him years before. Or at least I thought I had. When I was a kid. My father manufactured jewelry and had his shop on Fifty-second Street between Fifth and Madison. I used to come into the city from Long Island and run errands for him during the summer. And no matter where the delivery was supposed to go, I made sure I got there by going through the lobby of what was then called the RCA Building, 30 Rockefeller Plaza, with the hopes that maybe I would see Johnny Carson (whose show was upstairs) or some of the people from *That Was the Week That Was:* Buck Henry, Bob Dishy, David Frost—or Herb Sargent, who was the producer. I knew his name from the credits. As a young boy who wanted to be a TV writer someday, this was like hanging around outside of Yankee Stadium waiting to see the players going through to the clubhouse.

And now, now I was actually working with Herb Sargent. We gravitated toward each other (or should I say I forced myself upon him?) because my background was in joke writing and he was basically in charge of "Weekend Update," which was all about jokes. So I found my way into his office, and we would go through the newspapers together and write jokes for "Update." We made each other laugh. The silence was comfortable. And over time, the relationship grew deeper.

I believe that you choose people to fulfill roles in your life. And I cast Herb in the role not only of mentor but—there's a Jewish expression, *tzaddik*. A tzaddik is a just person. A person who embodies wisdom and integrity. I cast Herb in that role. He was the oldest person I knew, and I treated him with the kind of respect usually reserved for people who symbolize a person's private definition of truth—to the point where he was the one guy I knew that I couldn't lie to. And as the show became more successful and I started making a little money, he was the only one I didn't do drugs in front of. Still later on, when I was having problems with a girl I was going out with, I went to Herb, who had been married thirty-four times, for advice.

As a native New Yorker, I was also drawn to Herb because, to me, Herb was New York. But an older, more romantic New York that took place in black and white, like the kind of TV I grew up on and wanted to be a part of someday. Comedy with a conscience. And mindful of its power to influence. From the silly "Franco is still dead" jokes to softer ones about global warming, Herb taught us about the equal weight they carried.

When Lorne founded the show, he said that our generation was not being spoken to on television. So the politics on *SNL* were addressed to our generation—the baby boomers who had grown up watching television and went to Woodstock and thought it was absurd how Gerald Ford fell down so much. But here was Herb, a charter member of the older generation, who validated us. And encouraged us. And quite often led the way. What a curious hybrid he was—a man who was older than my father and at the same time younger than my Republican brother, but who wasn't preachy. Or controversial. But he lived in that place where he was writing about those things that he genuinely felt. Herb was grounded in his beliefs. So when he wrote, he wrote from within.

When I left New York and moved my family to Los Angeles, I knew my city was in good hands because Herb was there. And that I was still connected there because to know Herb Sargent was to be two degrees of separation from anyone on the planet. It was in his office that I'd met Mort Sahl and Herb Gardner and Art Buchwald and Avery Corman and Ed Koch and Bella Abzug. So in my mind, even though I was now living a full continent away, all I had to do was call Herb, remind him that I disliked L.A. as much as he did, and I was home. It was as simple as that—and all he asked in return was that I not join the Writers Guild, West.

So our relationship continued long-distance. I still tried hard to please him. Make him proud. I sent him a copy of anything I wrote or produced. Poor Herb, I actually sent him seventy-two videotapes of *It's Garry Shandling's Show* because his neighborhood didn't get Showtime in those years. I also sent him first drafts of plays, movies, magazine articles, and book manuscripts. He'd call and give me notes. And in those pre-Internet days he'd send reviews from New York papers. "Did you see this one about the Jon Lovitz special you did? Congratulations," he'd write. And when I'd get a bad review, he'd say, "Don't read *Time* magazine."

But after a while, for some reason, I lost touch with Herb. I'm not sure why. He might have been mad at me. I'm not sure of that either. For some reason I never asked. Never called to clear the air or simply reconnect. Years passed. Until I saw him at the memorial of a former *SNL* associate producer. Herb had been sick and now looked, well, now looked his age. It threw me. He'd never looked his age.

I moved my family back to New York and started calling him again. Tried to jump-start a friendship, make up for lost time. Calls were returned—but not as quickly as they once had been. I misjudged the situation and took it personally. Figured it to be nothing more than the vestiges of our estrangement. A sign that things between us were not yet back to where they were. But I was determined to remedy that. I wrote a novel. And when it came time to submit the names of people on the acknowledgments page, I mentioned Herb and tried my best to figure out how and when I would let him know about it. Should I send him the galleys and have him come across it? No, too much had transpired for me to give him that kind of homework. Should I call and tell him? Let him know outright how grateful and indebted I felt? No, I knew that would only serve to embarrass him. Make him blush. Herb hated recognition. Hated blushing. So I waited.

Decided to send him the published product once it came out and put a bookmark in the page that his name was on. It proved to be yet another miscalculation on my part. Herb died about a week before I had the chance to do so. I never got to tell him how much he meant to me. Somehow, some way, I hope he knows.

# Comic Dialogue

Upon graduation from college, I had to make a crucial choice about my future. Should I attend law school or pursue my long-time dream of becoming a comedy writer?

As it worked out, that decision was made for me by all twenty-three law schools I applied to. Feeling both rejected and relieved, I met Catskills comic Stu Cooper, who, over a cup of coffee at the Stage Deli, introduced me to my new profession.

—Basically, kid, there are six levels in show business.

—What do you mean?

—Like, you're either an unknown, or you're a semi-name, or you're a name, or you're a star, or you're a big star, or you're a superstar.

—I never thought of it in those terms.

—Oh, sure. And once you've been in the business for a while, you find that trying to get from one level to the next becomes your life. For instance, take Dickie Newfield. He's an unknown.

—Uh-huh.

—So is Dickie Pearl, Benny Diamond, Davey Opal, Jackie Stone . . .

—Right.

— . . . Davey Leigh, Lee Burton, Burt Lewis, Lou Stevens, Lew Burns, there's Dave Lenny and Lenny Martin and Marty Craig . . . All of them are unknown.

—Right.

—Marty Reynolds is unknown.

—I see.

—So's Lee Reynolds and Herbie Day and Jackie Dawn and Larry Storm . . .

—Got you.

—Then there's Mel Silvers, Burt Gold, Eddie Pines, Mickey Scott, Jackie Scott, Scotty Drake. . . . All of these guys are unknown.

—I see.

—You know what I mean?

—Sure.

—Oh, there's dozens of them.

—Right.

—Lenny Drake and Jimmy Robbins and Les Hanes . . .

—Right.

—Now, all of these guys are very good professional comics. They work the Catskills or they can come out and do twenty solid minutes in any room, whether it's opening for big stars like Steve and Eydie or even a superstar like Sammy.

—Couldn't they open for semi-names?

—An unknown opening for a semi-name? Who would come to see them?

—I'm not sure that I understand.

—Well, a superstar can have an unknown open for him because people will come to see a Liza or a Tom Jones or a
Humperdinck no matter who the opening act is. But semi-names
are only known by a few people, and unknowns aren't known
by anyone. So what would be the draw?

—Oh, I get you.

—You see, semi-names are semi-recognizable, because occasionally you can see us on a talk show or on TV commercials, so
we get paid slightly more in clubs—but we still have to share the
billing with a big star or superstar. Do you know what I mean?

—Right. Now, who are some of the semi-names?

—Well, there's me, Marty Blake, Morty Gunty, Mattie
Rose . . .

—Pat Henry?

—Oh, sure, Pat's a semi-name. But, you know, now that I
think of it, everyone knows that Pat's been opening for Sinatra
for so long that he could very well be a name already. Pat does
okay. So does Corbett.

—Corbett Monica?

—Yeah. Luckiest guy in the world. Ever see his act?

—No.

—Fair, at best. But people still know who he is from when he
was on *The Joey Bishop Show.*

—I remember that program.

—Joey threw him a bone, so Corbett's a name. But that's the
power of the tube. Red Buttons, Jan Murray, Morey Amster-
dam, Larry Storch, Phil Foster, Foster Brooks, Marty Ingels,
Marty Allen, Bernie Allen . . . Look at Nipsey Russell. Perfect
example. *Perfect* example. The guy gets up, right? He reads a
few poems. Okay, they're cute, but they're not going to change
the world. You know what I mean?

—Uh-huh.

—But he does a few game shows and a few Dean Martin roasts, so people know who he is, and that raises his price for what he gets in a club.

—I like Woody Allen.

—There's another example. He makes movies, they're cute— a lot of New York Jewish shtick—that's okay. But put him in a room in Vegas and nobody knows what he's talking about. The audience just sits there—he's too deep.

—God, Woody Allen's my idol.

—Hey, don't get me wrong. Woody's very clever. But, a night-club audience who pays fifty dollars a couple wants to laugh. They don't want to have to figure out what the guy is talking about and then decide if they should laugh. You know what I mean?

—Well . . .

—You can disagree with me if you want to.

—Sure. I know.

—But I'll tell you one thing—and you can take this from me, because if there's one thing I know, it's comedy—and I'll bet you that if you put Woody Allen in the same room with Jackie Gayle, Woody'd never know what hit him.

—Who's Jackie Gayle?

—The greatest lounge act in the history of Vegas. You know, you might think I'm crazy, but between you and me, I think he's even funnier than Shecky.

—Shecky Greene?

—Yep. I think Jackie's much funnier. But Shecky's got that Madame Butterfly routine that's a classic. That and "ca-ca on the moon"—twenty minutes of wall-to-wall screams.

—"Ca-ca on the moon"?

—Oh, you know that one.

—I do?

—That's the routine where Neil Armstrong had no place to go to the bathroom while he was in the spaceship, so that's why he was in such a hurry to land, so he could make a ca-ca on the moon.

—Oh . . . right.

—Shecky always had the best material, that's what made him. And that's what I need: some surefire material. Do you want to write for me?

—Sure. But . . .

—Well, you want to be a comedy writer, don't you?

—Sure. But I don't even know how to go about doing it.

—This stuff you sent me in the mail isn't bad.

—Really?

—It's a little sophomoric, but . . .

—Well, that was just some material that I wrote when I was in college.

—It's also a little bit too wordy. You've got to get to the punch lines quicker. The setups are way too long. Have you ever seen me work?

—No. . . . Well, I mean not recently. My parents used to take us on weekend trips to the Catskills, so of course I saw you then.

—I'm pretty frenetic onstage. I like to move around a lot. I like to play the room, the way Carter does.

—Jack Carter?

—Sure. Hey, let's face it—we're all doing Jack.

—Of course.

—So that's why I need a lot of quick one-line zingers. I never stand in one place long enough to do a setup joke. It'd break my rhythm.

—Okay. Is there any special subject you want me to write about?

—No, not really. Just so long as it's funny. That's all I care about.

—Okay.

—My audience likes to laugh at just about anything. Like marriage, or divorce, or in-laws, or a date coming to pick up your daughter, or the commercials they do on TV. You know what I mean?

—Sure. I'll do my best.

—Great. And if by some chance you can come up with a hook for me . . . Christ, that would get me to the next level, or even make me a star, so fast it'd make your head spin.

—What's a hook?

—An image. An identity. A shtick. It's something that'd let people know that "Stu Cooper—he's the guy who is such and such."

—Oh, I see.

—You know what I mean?

—I think so.

—Like Jack Benny's cheap—that's his hook—that's what made him. Alan King's angry, Gleason's fat, Hackett's got that speech impediment. . . . All the big stars have some hook, and that's how the audience knows them, and that's what I'm looking for.

—Right. Okay.

—Hey, it's not that easy. I'm real hard to find an attitude for. I'm forty-four, I don't have a big nose, and I look sort of handsome in my tuxedo—so the audience doesn't believe it when I make fun of myself. You know what I mean?

—Uh-huh . . .

—No one would believe that "I don't get no respect."

—Right.

—You know what I mean?

—Sure.

—That line is great for Rodney because he looks that way. But that could never work for me. I'm too classy-looking. You see, the audience has to believe that the comic could actually have those things that he's saying happen to him. To be someone that people remember, you got to be a believable character.

—I got you.

—Like, I have a friend, a comedian, named Larry Best. He does a very funny thing in his act: he pretends that he's eating an apple.

—Really.

—It's hysterical. He cups his hand and brings it up to his mouth and does these sound effects that are so funny, like he was actually biting into and chewing an apple. And the audience screams. And he goes on and on with these crunchy sounds and slurps to the point where you'd swear that the juice was actually dripping down his chin.

—Right.

—But as funny as it is, Larry's still unknown. Sure, people know that there's a guy around who does a very funny bit about eating an apple, but Larry never came up with a memorable character onstage to make people remember that Larry Best's the guy who eats the apple.

—I see.

—And it's been that way with him his whole career. Christ, I remember Larry before he was unknown.

—Huh?

—Oh, sure. I met Larry when he was first starting out.

—Oh.

—So it's tricky. How old are you?

—Twenty-two.

—Christ, I've been in this business since before you were born. I was nineteen when I started out. . . .

—Uh-huh.

—And I've had every big writer write for me at one time or other, and none of them have been able to capture me.

—Really?

—Oh, sure. They all wrote for me. Arnie Kogen, Arnie Rosen, Arnie Sultan, Larry Gelbart, Larry Rhine, Mel Tolkin, Mel Brooks, Neil Simon, Danny Simon . . .

—Neil Simon?

—Sure. As a matter of fact, I discovered him.

—Really?

—Sure. He started out just like you. They all did. They sold jokes here and there, and then they graduated to selling routines. And when their names got around, they started writing for more and more comics, and then when one of those comics caught a break and got a TV program, the way Caesar did, the comic would ask the writers to work on that show and that's how they all broke into TV.

—Wow. That's exactly what I want to do.

—You can do it.

—Really?

—Sure. Like, for example, you write for me or any of the other comics that are around—I can introduce you to all of them—and if one of us gets a show, you'd write for it.

—That'd be amazing. You know, being a TV comedy writer has always been my dream, ever since I used to watch the old *Dick Van Dyke Show.*

—Good program.

—Do you still speak with Neil Simon?

—Occasionally I call and he gives me a joke if I need it, but he's very busy. Do you have a car?

—No. I live with my parents, so I usually borrow theirs.

—Well, why don't you come up to the mountains with me one night this weekend? You can drive up to the house, have dinner with the family, and then you can come and watch me work.

—That would be great.

—Just pick a night. I'm at the Nevele on Friday, and I'm doing the late show at the Concord on Saturday.

—Well, I have work on Friday night, so I'll have to make it Saturday, if that's okay.

—Super. What kind of work do you do?

—Well, I have a B.A. in psychology, but now I'm just working part-time in a delicatessen on Long Island—until I can get things together a little bit.

—Oh, that's so funny.

—What's so funny?

—That's so funny—that your background in psychology helps you understand the pastrami before you slice it.

— . . . Right.

—Isn't that funny?

—Yeah . . . sure.

—Tell you what. I'm going to use that in my act tonight, and if it gets a laugh, I'll send you seven dollars. Then you'll really be a professional writer.

—But I didn't say that about the pastrami—you did.

—That's all right. I never would have thought of that gag if we didn't have this conversation.

—Oh. . . . Thanks.

—And I'll see you on Saturday and we'll take it from there.

—Great.

—I'm going into Vegas next month, and maybe you could come up with a couple of things by then.

—Sure.

—I'm opening for Tony Orlando, and I'd really like to knock 'em dead out there.

—Sure.

—Orlando's got that TV show coming up this summer and they're going to need comics, so I really want to show Tony's people what I can do.

—Sure.

—I'm especially interested in about five strong minutes. Something about jogging. Or sending the kids to camp. . . . Like I say, anything as long as it's funny. I want to do it in the spot where I usually do ca-ca on the moon.

—I thought Shecky Greene does ca-ca on the moon.

—Well, yeah. But we don't play the same places. So it doesn't hurt Shecky at all. And when I go into Vegas, I don't do it. That's why I need you to write me some material.

—Okay, Mr. Cooper.

—Stu.

—Sure, Stu.


AUGUST 1975

—Hello.

—Listen, did I wake you? It's Stu.

—No . . . no . . . that's okay. . . . What time is it?

—It's, let me look at my watch, it's eleven-thirty out here, so that would make it . . .

— . . . Two-thirty in the morning.

—Right, two-thirty New York time. Are you sure I didn't wake you?

—No, no. Is everything all right?

—Just super. Look, remember that inflation joke you wrote for me a few years ago?

—What joke was that?

—The one where I say that the price of meat is getting so bad that yesterday I stole a piece of flanken that had a street value of six thousand dollars.

—Right, I remember.

—Super joke. Well, I've been using that joke in my act, and it gets screams in the mountains, they just love it.

—Uh-huh.

—But I noticed that here in Vegas the joke just does okay. They like it here, but it doesn't play the way it does in front of Jews who know that flanken is boiled meat and that's what makes it a great joke.

—Right.

—So I find that the ones who know what *flanken* means scream when they hear the joke and the ones who don't know what the hell flanken is don't scream as hard.

—Right.

—I mean, they laugh, but not as hard as they would if they understood what it meant. You know what I mean?

—Sure.

—It's just too hip for this crowd. So what I did was change the joke around a little so that everyone out here would get it.

—Uh-huh.

—So what I did was, I switched it around to "the price of meat is getting so bad that yesterday I stole a pot roast that had a street value of six thousand dollars."

—Uh-huh.

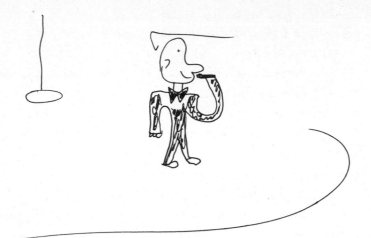

—Isn't that funny?

—Oh, yeah. . . . It's great.

—Look, you and I know that it's still the flanken-joke for-mula, but this way it plays better for these goyim out here.

—Right.

—So what happened was, I wanted to try it out before I did it onstage. Just to test it, you know?

—Uh-huh.

—As a matter of fact, I called you earlier to tell you the joke.

—I was working tonight.

—Right. So I'm out here opening for Tony Martin and Cyd Charisse, and we were having dinner, and I told Tony the joke. Well, when I tell you that he started laughing, but I mean tears were coming out . . .

—Really?

—And Cyd, you know Cyd never laughs . . .

—Uh-huh.

—You know Tony and Cyd, don't you?

—No.

—Well, everyone knows that Cyd doesn't laugh . . .

—Oh.

— . . . but when I told her this joke I got worried, because I thought she was going to have a stroke from laughing so hard.

—That's great.

—It's a super joke, isn't it?

—Oh, yeah.

—I called Vic, and he loved it, too.

—That's great.

—Freddy didn't laugh, but I didn't let it bother me. I figured that was his problem. You know how he gets.

—Right.

—You know what I mean?

—Sure.

—So I won't let that bother me. I bumped into Jackie Eagle in a coffee shop, and he also thought it was a super joke.

—Uh-huh.

—And he also said that Freddy was jealous and that I shouldn't let it bother me.

—Right.

—So what's doing with you?

—Everything's fine. This job on *Saturday Night Live* is going real good. I'm learning how to write sketches, and today we filmed a—

—Super. Did you hear about Pat Crane?

—Who?

—Catskills comic. Does this thing about having an Irish grandmother.

—Uh-huh.

—You know who I'm talking about?

—Yeah. I met him at . . .

—He died. Was killed in a car crash on his way home from a job.

—Oh my God.

—Yeah, it happened a few weeks ago. It was terrible. He was only forty-six. Had a wife, three kids. . . .

—I'm really sorry to hear that.

—I know. It's a real tragedy.

—God.

—I'm doing his bit about farting in an elevator.

—What?

—I asked his wife, Barbara, and she said it would be all right.

—Wow.

—Which reminds me, I must give her a call when I get back to New York. I haven't spoken to her since the funeral, because I left for Vegas the next day.

—Wait a second. You mean to tell me that at Pat Crane's funeral you asked his wife if you could do his bit about farting in an elevator?

—No, of course not.

—But . . .

—I asked her on the way back from the cemetery.

—Oh.

—Look, my daughter Leslie's going to be sixteen, so we're giving her a big sweet-sixteen party.

—Uh-huh.

—Do you think that there's a routine in that?

—There could be. . . .

—You know, with the invitations, and now she's old enough to date, or the records that kids listen to. . . . There must be some routine in there somewhere.

—Sure.

—You know, if you can think of it, that's where I can use some punching up in my act. Like I do that routine about the names of the different musical groups.

—Right.

—Like I do that thing where I say that the musical groups today have the strangest names, like "Crosby, Stills, Nash and Young—what kind of name is that? When I first heard it, I thought it was the name of a law firm."

—Right.

—It's a super joke, but it only works to the hipper crowds. The young people like it.

—Uh-huh.

—Or I say: "The Jefferson Airplane—what kind of name is that? Did you ever hear their music? I'll tell you one thing, that's one airplane I wouldn't mind seeing hijacked."

—Right.

—It's a super joke. You have to think about it for a second, but it works.

—Uh-huh.

—So that's what I could use more of—names of musical groups. It's good material for television, you know what I mean?

—Sure.

—It's clean, and appeals to the young people—which is the audience that TV's trying to reach.

—Right.

—Look, I know you're busy with your show and everything, but could you do me a favor and just jot down some funny names of musical groups for me?

—Okay.

—It's a funny idea, isn't it?

—Oh, yeah.

—Look, I'll let you go back to sleep. . . .

—Okay.

—Sorry I woke you.

—That's all right.

— . . . but off the top of your head, could you think of a funny name of a musical group?

—Uh . . . the Grateful Dead?

—No. . . . It's not bad, but the routine works a lot better when I use the names of actual groups.

—But . . .

—Look, I know you're tired. So give it some thought, and I'll call you when I get back to New York.

—Okay.

—Good night.


FEBRUARY 1980

—I just can't believe that I'm fifty years old.

—I know. But you don't look it.

—Really?

—No. No way.

—Thanks. . . . Hey, it was nice of all the boys to come, wasn't it?

—Sure was.

—That's why we made the party today, so most of the boys wouldn't be working.

—Right.

—There's very few jobs on Sunday afternoons, unless it's a special affair or something. The only one who couldn't make it is Davey Kent. He's entertaining on a cruise, so he won't be back till Tuesday.

—What are those cruises like?

—They fly you down to Miami, you get on the boat, you visit the islands, and you just have to do two shows.

—On the boat?

—Yeah. And all of your accommodations are taken care of. It's not too bad. The money's okay—especially if you can pick up a night or two playing one of those condominiums before you fly back from Miami.

—You don't do those cruises though, do you?

—Me? No. It's not a career move. You know what I mean?

—Sure.

—I used to do them, when the kids were younger. We'd take them with us, and that'd be our vacation. . . . Hey, can I get you another drink?

—No, thanks. I'm okay.

—Len Bernie's funny, isn't he?

—He was the one who was making the jokes about everyone's gifts, right?

—Ain't he a riot? He does that at every party. It's like a ritual. Do you realize that people buy presents and actually try to predict what Len is going to say about them?

—God . . .

—That's right. If he were only that funny onstage. For years we've been trying to convince him that he should do some material about gifts and gift giving, but it's like talking to a wall. That's his son over there. Vale. Good-looking kid, isn't he?

—Vale?

—Yeah. He goes with my daughter Leslie. For about two years now.

—Vale Bernie?

—Well, actually his last name is Katzenbaum. Len calls himself Len Bernie as a stage name.

—Vale Katzenbaum? What kind of a name is that?

—Oh, it's a long story. But in a nutshell what happened was that Len, who was struggling for years as an unknown—this was in the early sixties—was asked to be the opening act for Jerry Vale when Jerry went into the Copa. Jerry Vale was a real big star back then—now he's probably just a name—but at that time he was playing Vegas and headlining in the biggest nightclubs, so this was like a real big break for Len because it could give him all sorts of exposure he never had before.

—Uh-huh.

—So Len opens for Jerry, and he's a big hit. He just killed 'em. I remember there was this big party afterward, Sinatra was there, Dean Martin, Sammy—all of Jerry's friends as well as Len and his wife, Sylvia, who was pregnant at the time. Well, you know how those parties get—I think it was at Toots Shor's— and everyone's having a great time, and Jerry comes up to Len and hugs him and says that he was great and that he wants Len to open for him when he goes into Vegas and when he tours that summer. Well, Len was beside himself. He picked up the tab for the party, and a few days later, when Sylvia gave birth, they named the baby Vale.

—Why didn't they just name him Jerry?

—Well, Len wanted Jerry to know that the baby was really named after him and not Jerry Van Dyke, who was also a good friend of Len's.

—How did the tour go?

—He didn't get it. We all told Len that you can't count on anything in this business until the contracts are signed, but you know how Len has a tendency to get carried away. So how are you doing?

—Fine. The show's still going strong, but I'm starting to get a little bored with sketch writing. I think I'd like to try . . .

—Sure. Hey, you know what I need is . . . I'm sorry, I thought you were finished.

—Well, I was just saying that I'd like to try my hand at writing something more challenging than a sketch. My dream is to write a movie and have it directed by someone like Coppola.

—Who?

—Francis Ford Coppola. . . . He did *The Godfather.*

—Oh, yeah, yeah, yeah, yeah, yeah. He's a clever kid. . . . You know, that's what I wanted to talk to you about.

—What's that?

—Well, you know the piece in my act where I talk about replacing all the items in my lost wallet.

—Yeah.

—It's funny. Isn't it?

—Oh, yeah. . . . Very funny.

—Do you think that it could be a TV series?

—What?

—I'll tell you, it's been so successful for me that some people are starting to know me because of that bit. You know, in the mountains I'm actually starting to be known as the comic who lost his wallet. It sounds crazy, but this could be my hook.

—Uh-huh.

—It's a funny image, isn't it?

—Oh, yeah. . . . Very funny.

—Well, do you think that you could develop it into a series for me?

—I don't know. A series about losing a wallet?

—The series could be about anything, but I'd play the guy next door who can't drive anywhere because his license was in the wallet . . .

—Well . . .

— . . . and I can't even buy a new wallet because my credit cards were in the lost one, and I can't get any money because my check-cashing card was also in the lost wallet.

—Uh-huh.

—There's a million things we can see me do or not do because I lost my wallet. Why don't you give it some thought?

—Sure.

—I'll tell you, it could be fun. And let's face it—I've seen a lot of worse ideas made into television series.

—You got a point there.

—Are you sure you don't want me to freshen your drink?

—On second thought, why don't you?

—That's the boy.

## JUNE 1983

—Hello.

—Hi, Stu, how you doing?

—Isn't that something? I was just talking about you.

—Really?

—Yeah, I was going to call and ask you how the wedding went.

—Oh, it was great. Thanks.

—Your parents, Robin, everyone have a good time?

—Oh, yeah.

—Good, good. . . . And the band? They were good?

—Oh, they were fine.

—I'm glad. I'm sorry we weren't able to make it, but like I said, I had to be away on a job and I just couldn't swing it.

—No, no, I understand. How *did* the cruise go, anyway?

—Just great. You know those things. A week on the boat, I

did a couple of shows—it was real easy. Everything got screams. Hey, listen, is this funny? "Milton Berle was the only infant I know whose foreskin was used to cover the infield at Yankee Stadium." Is that a funny joke?

—Yeah.

—You like it?

—Yeah, it's funny.

—The Friars are roasting Paul Williams next week, and I'm on the dais, but before I get into my Paul Williams material, you know how I always like to shpritz whoever else is there.

—Uh-huh.

—And Berle is going to be the roastmaster, so I figured that I'd zing him with that one.

—Right.

—It's a funny joke, isn't it?

—Oh, yeah. Very funny.

—I think it'll get a laugh. I got it from this kid who's here with me now. He's just breaking in. He's only twenty-four years old, but he's got some cute ideas, so I'm trying to help him out. He reminds me of you a little.

—Uh-huh.

—Look, maybe you could meet me for a cup of coffee or something and we could discuss the Paul Williams material?

—Okay.

—I really think that it's all there, but maybe you can come up with a gag or two to punch it up.

—Sure.

—I was telling this young writer that you were writing gags just like he's doing until you caught that break and got on TV.

—Right.

—So you want to get together?

—Sure.

—How does Tuesday sound?

—Tuesday's the only day I have a problem with. Can you make it Wednesday?

—Sure, Wednesday's no problem. What do you have doing on Tuesday?

—Well, that's actually why I called. You see, I wrote this movie script that's going into production, and on Tuesday I have a—

—Okay, Wednesday's fine. The roast isn't until Friday, so I'll still have time to go over whatever we come up with over coffee.

—Sure, but listen, I got to tell you—

—I'd like to do well at the roast. It doesn't pay anything, but it's a good career move. I figure if I do good enough, maybe Paul will give me some weeks on his next tour. That's what happened to Freddy last time when they roasted Ben Vereen.

—Look, Stu. I have something to tell you that concerns you.

—Really?

—Yes. I wrote this movie, and I want you to be in it.

—You're kidding.

—No, I'm not. That's what I'm trying to tell you. Tuesday I have a meeting with the casting director, and I want to talk to him about you.

—Geez, I can't believe it. A movie . . . What's it about?

—Well, basically it's about the relationship between a young writer and a comic.

—Right. . . .

—And, what can I tell you, as the years go by they sort of grow apart comedically, and really don't have that much in common on a professional level anymore. You know what I'm saying?

—Sure.

—But the two of them still keep in touch because they're

friends and because the kid stills feels grateful to the comic for giving him his first break and helping make his dream come true.

—Super. Super.

—You like it?

—Are you kidding? It sounds just super.

—Thanks. Well, anyway, Kevin Kline might play the writer who's going to eventually create a role that could help make the comic's dream come true.

—Uh-huh. . . .

—Because the comic is . . . How should I say this? He's the kind of guy who should be happy—like he's got a beautiful home, a great family, and he makes a lot of money opening for all sorts of headliners.

—Uh-huh . . .

—But he's the kind of guy who'll never be really happy until he himself becomes a household name—which is what the writer's going to try to do by creating this role for this friend. Do you know what I'm saying?

—Oh, sure I do.

—Well, what do you think?

—It's super. It really is. It really sounds like a winner.

—Thanks.

—Now, what part were you thinking of having me play in the movie?

—Well . . . uh, I thought it'd be great if you played the part of the comic.

—Really? Hmmm . . .

—Is something wrong?

—Well, the problem is that I'm not an actor.

—So?

—So I can't see how the hell I can play a guy like that.

—But . . .

—I mean, look, I know the kind of comic that you're talking about. Christ, I must know a thousand of them. But I don't think it'd be believable if I did it. You know what I mean?

—Well . . .

—Look, I'm really flattered that you asked me. Really I am.

—Uh-huh . . .

—Hey, I have an idea. Why don't you actually use one of those comics? You know, some unknown like Dickie Curtis, or Lenny Bates, or Joey Rush? Some guy who can actually play himself? Have you thought of that?

—Well . . .

—Christ, that would be a hell of a shot for someone like that.

—Right.

—You should consider it.

—Okay.

—Hey, look, thanks again for thinking of me.

—Sure.

—And I'll see you on Wednesday to talk about the Paul Williams roast. Okay?

—Sure.

—What do you say, two o'clock at the Stage Deli?

—That'll be fine.

—So I'll see you then?

—Uh-huh.

—Super.

## Bad Exit Strategy

Allow me to begin by saying that I'm basically a good guy. I'm a faithful husband and loving father who tries his best to be a good neighbor in the small New Jersey suburb we live in. Despite all best intentions, however, I do admit that I am not above occasional mishaps—human errors that range from inadvertent oversights to wrongheaded miscalculations. But if pressed to recall a moment where I plummeted to my lowest depth of civil behavior, the time when my chosen exit strategy was, at best, atrocious, it would undoubtedly be what took place about ten summers ago in our town's swimming pool.

It was an August afternoon. The temperature was in the nineties and our kids were getting antsy, so we decided to take them to the local swim club. The Olympic-sized pool was crowded with similar-thinking neighbors who were seeking relief from the oppressive heat. The time soon came, however, when I found myself in need of relief of my own. That's right, I had to pee and was faced with the familiar decision of whether to leave the pool and endure the hot cement of the pool's perimeter on my barefooted way to what was traditionally an unkempt men's room or simply stay put and add a little water of my own to my surroundings.

I opted for the latter with no knowledge whatsoever that the town was trying an experiment where they put a chemical in the pool that, when combined with the acidic property of urine, turned a reddish color, which, in effect, acted as a billboard proclaiming, "THIS DISGUSTING PERSON JUST PEED IN OUR LOVELY POOL!" What followed was even more horrifying, as I had no way of knowing that the rather heavyset woman who was next to me, the one to whom I pointed to let our community know that it was indeed she who made a liquid donation to where they were bathing before I scampered away in a cowardly attempt to put as much distance between us as possible, was a local candidate for mayor. That what I was actually doing was telling a significant segment of the town's voting population that this sweet, grandmotherly woman who was running on a "town beautification" platform had just sullied these very waters with a beverage that she had drunk earlier and was now personally recycling into the pool that they and their loved ones were playing Marco Polo in.

The elections were held that November, and she lost by nine votes. Whether those nine people were at the pool that day and this episode influenced their decision is a question I cannot answer. Nor can I tell you with any degree of certainty that if she was elected mayor, she wouldn't have eventually ridden that wave of popularity to higher offices in the county, state, or, God help me, the United States Senate, had I not snuffed out her political career. All I do know is that about a year later, I saw her at the crowded deli counter of our local supermarket, said, "I am so, so sorry," and handed her the much lower number I was holding before scurrying away as quickly as if she had just peed in a swimming pool.

# The Enchanted Nectarine

In 1979 I ate a nectarine that I still think about.

It was August. August 2 to be exact. My girlfriend and I were getting engaged, and a show I'd written material for, *Gilda Live,* was about to begin its run on Broadway. Life was good. And was made that much sweeter by a purchase I'd made at a Columbus Avenue grocery on my way to rehearsal. A nectarine. China's contribution to the world of fruit. And while this writer does not regard himself adequately gifted to describe the glory of that mutant peach with hairless skin, let's just say that the moment I bit into it, I instantly forgave God for all the wars and sufferings he'd previously turned his back on—figuring he was busy making this amazing nectarine while all that other stuff was happening. This taste of heaven, which caused me to wonder whether, at the next round of SALT, the Soviet Union would think twice about invading Afghanistan if Jimmy Carter were to feed Leonid Brezhnev a nectarine like this one just before their little chat got under way. Whether Leonid would, instead, take one bite, immediately drop to the floor in a squatting position, and hold Carter's hands as they kicked their heels in the jubilant Cossack dance from the wedding scene in *Fiddler on the Roof*.

But the wonders of this nectarine did not stop there, however, as my other senses, apparently envious of the festival the taste buds were attending, shifted into a higher gear and became more receptive to the offerings of the city street's colors, music, and smells that they were previously too self-involved to savor.

Yes, all that was right with the world was embodied in that single nectarine, whose only fault was that it wasn't the size of a basketball so its majesty could be shared by entire neighborhoods over the course of several weeks. As it was, I now was in the process of sucking whatever juices still remained in the strands clinging to its pit when I entered the Winter Garden Theater and learned of a tragedy—first from a stagehand, then verified by everyone else. Thurman Munson, the New York Yankees catcher and team captain, had died in a plane crash. The heart of the lineup as well as the dominant spirit of their clubhouse lost his life while practicing takeoffs and landings in the Cessna he'd bought so he could spend days off with his family in Canton, Ohio.

A city of fans was instantly bound by shock. Disbelief. Raw emotions were soon followed by tributes. The catcher's position left empty as the Yankees took the field for their next game . . . The scoreboard photo of Munson, his frizzy hair peeking out from beneath his cap, towering over a tearful Reggie Jackson in right field . . . A young widow with three small children at a televised funeral.

I'd never met Thurman Munson, but I mourned the loss. Selfishly, I was going to miss his presence on the team he personified. Their first captain since the legendary Lou Gehrig. Emblazoned on the tail of the doomed Cessna was the same number that was stitched on his jersey, NY15. A true Yankee to his untimely end.

I didn't idolize Thurman Munson—perhaps because I was now twenty-nine years old and supposedly past the age of regarding ballplayers with the same awe as I did Mickey Mantle and Sandy Koufax while growing up. Then again, those players were bigger than the game itself, performing with a grace that elevated the acts of hitting and throwing cowhide to an art form. This was not the case with Thurman Munson, whose play was regularly described by adjectives such as *scrappy, gruff,* and *combative.* Whereas I don't have a single memory of Willie Mays having a spot of dirt on his uniform, Thurman was the blue-collar counterpart who wallowed in his attempts to protect home plate or dive into the stands to catch a foul ball. His every move gave the appearance of an effort. Unbridled exertion. Thurman's demeanor was abrupt and coarse. He was stout and hairy, and on no planet in any universe would he be considered handsome. Yet, this was his attraction. Why he was crudely lov-

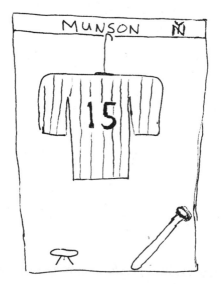

able. Ralph Kramden with shin guards. A common laborer who toiled for a paycheck. Who loved his family. And his life. And most probably appreciated a good nectarine. Devoured it with abandon. Relished every fleck that didn't get caught in his droopy moustache. And slobbered the juices that hadn't already spilled onto the front of his already soiled shirt.

Did Thurman Munson like nectarines? Was it possible that the bulge in this tough guy's cheek was not a chaw of tobacco but, indeed, a pit? I had no way of finding out. I knew none of his teammates, and the few sportswriters I was friendly with thought I was kidding when I asked. So the question was quickly assigned to the same part of my brain where other former curiosities like "Would Jesus have thought Good Friday was an appropriate name for the day he was crucified?" and "Do fat people use more toilet paper?" were filed.

Then, some years later, I met Thurman's wife, Diana. A friend of mine took me to a reception the night before Old-Timers Day at the stadium. I got to see some of my childhood heroes, now elderly men in shirts and ties who no longer looked like baseball players but like elderly men in shirts and ties. Sensitive to both their and my need for them to be young again, I found myself picturing these gentlemen as they once looked on baseball cards—a white lie that no one in the room seemed to mind. When I was introduced to Mrs. Munson, however, more than anything, I wanted to ask if her late husband liked nectarines, but I knew my question would be a reflection on the person I was a guest of and the collateral damage could have been disastrous if it was deemed inappropriate or, more likely, idiotic.

So while I know that it would be a far better ending to this tale if I said that by the end of the evening my curiosity swelled to the brink of eruption, causing me to dash out into the parking lot, catching up to her just as she reached her car, excuse myself, ask if Thurman liked nectarines, and that she took a moment to orient herself before a wide smile appeared on her face as she recalled the memory and said, "Why yes, Thurman loved nectarines"—I cannot honestly say that is what happened. Nor can I say that to this very day whenever I bite into an amazing nectarine, I think about Thurman Munson. Hell no. If that kind of sappiness even makes this oftentimes overly sentimental wordsmith cringe with horror, my guess is that Thurman would use it as an excuse to come back from the dead to beat the shit out of me, and he would be justified in doing so. In fact, there's an excellent chance that I would join him in giving me a sound thrashing. That being said, I cannot remember eating as good a nectarine since that day.

# My Daughter Lindsay

I write. This is what I do. I take words and place them in an order that will hopefully hold your interest when set down on a page or when uttered by human voices on a stage or a screen. Why do I do this? I have no choice. I'm a writer. I was born this way. And while I realize that there are far worse genetic conditions that a person can be afflicted with on the journey from one end of life to the other, the fact remains that writing is what I do because a writer is what I am.

I belong to that particular breed whose work is unlike any job where it's necessary to remain detached from private concerns, emotional stirrings, and both painful and happy memories so as not to be distracted from effectively performing whatever task one's work requires. My work suggests that I do just the opposite. My work suggests that I dwell on these events and their associated feelings for the purpose of infusing them into the reality of my characters and the world that my work deposits them in. Tone? Important but secondary. Important because the sensibility of the piece, and the craftsmanship employed in its presentation, will ultimately affect how well a story is received by an audience whose only agenda is to enjoy themselves. Secondary because whether it's comedic or dramatic, romantic or aloof, maudlin or cynical, the attitude of the selected words is but a veneer unless a relatable truth is at the core.

This does present a problem, however. Because to have ready access to the memory of feelings, the writer must shed layers of protective psychological buildup. And in doing so, he must expose himself in such a way that criticism can be extremely hurtful.

Recently I got hurt. No, allow me to revise that. Recently, I got destroyed. Beaten to a pulp. Hammered. Nailed. Kicked in the groin. The stomach. The face. Chewed up. Spit out. And left for dead.

Recently I wrote a movie. It was a simple tale that I felt passionate about. Based on a simple book I'd written, which I also felt passionate about. But when the movie came out, the critics hated it. With a passion. Consequently, the words they chose to describe my words were words like "bad," "really bad," and "What the hell was he thinking?"

Hurtful? Quite. But what I had written was, at the very least, well intentioned. Operating on the assumption that a child, at one point or another, may feel unappreciated by his folks, I wrote a fantasy where a young boy named North embarks on a worldwide search for the perfect parents before coming to the conclusion that his parents, despite their shortcomings, are the best for him. I liked the idea. And I still do. It's light and it's fun, but if people, in their professional judgment, do not care for the way the idea was executed, this is their prerogative. If, in their estimation, the words I chose do not effectively deliver the desired message, laughs, or tears, not only is it their job to say so but it's also possible that they are right. I'm only human. I make mistakes. Maybe I should have chosen different words. Or the same words but in a different order. Or the same words but in a different language. Or perhaps I somehow stumbled upon a curious phenomenon of chemistry where perfectly innocuous words, when placed in the order I put them in, suddenly stink to high heaven.

Whatever the case, as the script's author I accepted responsibility for its merit and only wished that I could apologize to anyone who was disappointed by the effort. But as a human being with feelings, I was stunned when some reviewers deployed phrases like "bad writer," "very bad writer," and "He calls himself a writer?" in mounting an attack that ventured beyond what I *did* to what I *am*.

This confused me, and it hurt. Badly. Weren't these reviews written by writers, brethren, who hailed from my own gene pool? So why were they taking words, the lifeblood of our species, and using them as weapons against one of their own? The security in thinking that my extended family of wordsmiths would, like any family, settle its differences quietly within itself was now shattered as public humiliation became compounded by feelings of betrayal and exclusion.

Shock gave way to paralysis, and I couldn't write. Few noticed. Banks stayed open, children weren't sent home from school, and the flag in front of our post office remained at full mast. But for a guy whose mom still shows old home movies of him as a three-year-old shouting the words "A writer!" while dancing on the lap of an odd-smelling uncle who asked him what he wanted to be when he grew up, this was sad. Well, think about it. What other way is there to describe the sight of someone who every morning just sat and stared, in catatonic horror, at yet another page that his words seemed desperate to be re-

moved from, as if they no longer enjoyed being in each other's company?

Unfortunately, many well-meaning people only served to aggravate the situation. Some friends and siblings felt too awkward to call, but their silence said a lot. And some of the ones I did hear from, well . . .

—Hello.

—Don't read *Time* magazine.

—Dad?

—You get *Time* magazine?

—Yeah. . . .

—You get this week's issue?

—It just came.

—Well, whatever you do, don't read pages 74, 75, and the top of 77.

—Why not?

—Because they really knock your ass around pretty good.

—Oh. . . .

—But on 76 there's a full-page ad for Subaru, so that one's safe.

—Oh. . . .

—Tell me, just so I know, what kind of circulation does a magazine like this have?

—I really don't know, Dad.

—Approximately. A million?

—No, more.

—A billion?

—No, I'd say around seven million.

—So what we're saying is that approximately seven million strangers now think these things about you.

—Well . . .

—Because I'll tell you, it's not easy for a parent to read something like this about their child.

—Uh-huh . . .

—I mean, for me it wasn't as bad. I'm a man so maybe I have tougher skin . . .

—Uh-huh . . .

—But as far as your mother is concerned, I think she's gonna have to change butchers.

—Why?

—Resnick made a comment.

—Your butcher made a comment about the movie?

—To Lillian Fein.

—What did he say?

—Don't ask.

—Dad . . .

—Alan, the man is an idiot. He can barely put two words together without stopping for directions. So why aggravate yourself with what that fat meat shlepper thinks. Okay?

—Okay.

—He said that you were "banal, sophomoric, and stunningly devoid of mirth, wit, and social redemption."

—Resnick, the idiot butcher, said that to Lillian Fein?

—Yeah, and you know the mouth on her.

—Resnick saw the movie?

—I doubt it. That cretin wouldn't leave his house if it was on fire, let alone to go pay to see a movie.

—Well, then how could he say . . . ?

—He was quoting one of the reviews.

—He was?

—Of course.

—Oh . . .

—I think the *Post*.

—Oh, so the *Post* gave a bad review, too?

—Brutal.

—Oh . . .

—I never read anything so malicious and hateful.

—Oh . . .

—But *Time* magazine is worse.

I was bombarded by similar accounts, and much to my horror, all strategies to remain inaccessible failed miserably. Even my answering machine, long considered a reliable shield for staving off unwanted information, was guilty of treason. Screening calls merely subjected me to a shyster neighbor's battle cry to "sue that bastard who called you those things in the *News*" at a decibel level that reverberated throughout the room in which I was already cowering. And when I did venture outdoors, I came to despise the insistent flashing of the little red light that taunted my return with condolences like the one from a snide high school nemesis who just wanted to say hi and that he was still going to take his children to see the movie despite the fact that "the paper down here in Charleston called you a . . . wait a second, let me find it . . . oh, here it is . . . 'a talentless perpetrator of meaningless drivel' . . . because all of us old Hewlett Bluejackets teammates still should be there to support one another."

Reeling from this fusillade of critical assaults, I was in no way prepared for the knockout punch, which was conveyed to me during an unscheduled encounter in a local supermarket with someone whom I had no choice but to regard as a credible source.

—Alan?

—Yes?

—Are you okay?

—Huh?

—You look terrible.

—Oh, I'm all right. How are you, Rabbi Freiling?

—Alan, what's wrong? Is anyone sick?

—No, everyone's fine.

—Is it the reviews of your film?

— . . . Yeah. I guess so.

—Terrible. Just terrible.

—You know, I tried my best . . .

—Of course you did.

—And if I failed, okay . . .

—Absolutely.

—But it's still just a movie. . . .

—Right.

—Yet a lot of these people are ranting like I committed some kind of war crime.

—Worse.

—Huh?

—I'm sorry. Pretend I didn't say anything. My love to Robin and the kids.

—No, wait a second.

—Look, I see how upset you already are. . . .

—Please tell me.

— . . . Look, the day your movie opened I just happened to be speaking to a colleague of mine who's quite active over at the Simon Wiesenthal Center.

—Right . . .

—And one topic led to another, you know . . .

—Right.

—And he knows that you're a congregant of mine . . .

—Right . . .

—And he had seen the papers . . .

—Right . . .

—And then one topic led to another again . . .

—Right . . .

—And then somehow, I can't recall the exact flow of our conversation, but somehow he started comparing the reviews that you got for *North* . . .

—Right . . .

—With the ones that Hitler got for *Mein Kampf.*

—He what?

—And, apparently, Hitler did better.

—Give me a break, Rabbi Freiling.

—You know, by and large.

—You mean to tell me that a fairy tale that reaffirms the ideals of a warm, loving, close-knit family didn't do as well as a very real, calculated plan for Germany to achieve its destiny as the master race by virtue of the systematic elimination of millions of innocent human beings in death camps?

—Hey, I'm quoting a colleague.

—But how's that possible?

—Well, obviously none of the American critics were in agreement with Hitler's philosophies.

—Right . . .

—In fact, until the Third Reich actually came into power, in most circles *Mein Kampf* was dismissed as the megalomaniacal illusions of an incarcerated madman.

—Okay . . .

—But still, none of them said that Hitler was a bad writer.

Perhaps it was his delivery. Or the setting. Perhaps if my spiritual leader had spoken the same exact words atop his pulpit where his outstretched arms seemed to be appealing to the heavens, instead of surrounded by a sea of Chips Ahoy! in aisle #6 of Safeway, they would've had more of an inspirational impact on me as opposed to putting me in the state that I was in.

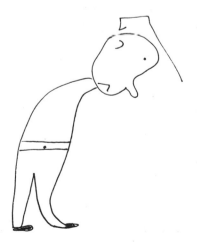

For me, depression has always been a moody guest that stays until I get bored with pampering it. When I was younger and had a dearth of responsibilities and an overabundance of spare time, I was a more indulgent host who actually welcomed the condition as an old friend. It was a comfortable and able protector from the world outside myself until I felt ready to retake my place among the living. But today, like any so-called adult, I find the temptation to withdraw frustrated by the demands and needs of those who depend on my being strong.

My wife and I have three children. There names are Adam, Lindsay, and Sari. And like all parents, I love all of them the same. There are no favorites, though each of them has traits that are favorites of mine. Adam is thirteen years old, a wonderful athlete, and I love the fact that he hides his *Playboy* magazines in the same places that I used to. Lindsay came next, and for the first four years of her life I loved the way her songs and giggles filled our home with the unbridled joy of a child confident that she was loved. That's why, when Sari was born, it was important that Lindsay be reassured that she was not being replaced as Daddy's little girl. Suddenly a middle child, Lindsay proudly accepted congratulations on her promotion to big sister. But one couldn't help but notice how her eyes seemed to wonder if this was happening because she had somehow failed in her role as recipient of all the attention that Sari was now getting.

This issue was addressed during those special times that Lindsay and I set aside for each other. We danced in the living room before I left for work in the morning. Every Saturday we drove to the same Chinese restaurant for a "secret lunch" to discuss, at length, the events of the previous week in our respective worlds of adulthood and kindergarten. And when *The Nutcracker* came to town, I put on a blazer, Lindsay wore a dress, and we had a "date."

The stuff between a father and a daughter is a melody of unconditional firsts. He's the first man to hold her hand. Smile when he sees her. Give her flowers. Hug her when she cries. For me, Lindsay was the first girl I had no trouble singing to in public. Whose crib I hung out by just to watch her sleep. Who I allowed to stand on my shoulders so she'd get a better view of Snoopy at a Thanksgiving Day parade. I also wrote little notes to Lindsay that I put in her lunch box. Last year, while sitting at her desk at Open School Night, I came upon an envelope in which she kept all of these little notes. And tacked to a nearby bulletin board was her composition about how she wanted to be a writer when she grew up.

A connection had been made, and needless to say, I felt great. But the infatuation was mutual. And still is. Lindsay is a beautiful and popular fifth-grader who plays soccer, takes dance lessons, loves the Beatles, and writes poems when it rains. She believes in the tooth fairy but once left a dollar under her little sister's pillow when I forgot to do so. And she wrote numerous letters to Dennis Byrd, the injured New York Jets football player, when the news said that he might never walk again. We play cards in the kitchen and duets on the piano, and we both cry every time we see Steve Martin play basketball with his daughter the night before her wedding in *Father of the Bride.*

Yes, the bond is sweet and real, and it wasn't difficult for her to detect the fraudulence her father felt when he was hurting yet tried to appear strong to his family.

—Hi, Daddy.

—Hey, Linz.

—Why are you so quiet?

—Oh, I'm just sitting here thinking.

—Are you writing something?

—No, not really. I'm just sitting here thinking.

—. . . Dad?

—Yeah, Linz?

—If I tell you something, do you promise not to punish me?

—What?

—I mean it. There's something I really want to tell you, but I don't want to get in trouble for it.

—You won't.

—Promise?

—Promise.

—Okay. Ready?

—Yeah.

—Fuck 'em.

—Excuse me?

—Those people who are saying those things about you and the movie. Fuck 'em.

—Lindsay . . .

—Well, what would you say to me if I did a project for school and my teacher gave me a bad grade?

—Well, I'm not sure that I'd say f—

—You would ask me if I tried my hardest, because that's the best that anyone could ask for, right?

—Right, but . . .

—So that's what happened to you. Only difference is that instead of a teacher, you got bad grades from newspapers and magazines and that guy on Channel 4 and . . .

—What guy on Channel 4?

—Dad, it doesn't matter. Didn't you once tell me that Angie Dickinson never sold any of her poems while she was alive but she kept on writing them anyway because deep down she still thought they were good poems and that she was a good writer?

—Emily Dickinson.

—Whatever . . . Dad, *you're* a good writer. A lot of people think that. Even that guy on Channel 4 said that you're a good writer.

—He did?

—Uh-huh. He just thought that you should have your head examined so you won't write anything like that again.

—I see.

—Wow, you actually smiled.

— . . . Linz?

—Yeah?

—Do you still like to write?

—Uh-huh.

—You do?

—Sure.

—Why?

—Because it makes me feel comfortable.

—It does?

—Yeah.

Perhaps it was her delivery. Or the setting. Or maybe the time was just right for me to be receptive to something obvious when offered by someone special.

As for my daughter's language, well, I promised that I wouldn't punish her for her choice of words, so I didn't. And though I probably could've busted her on "respect your elders" charges, she got away with a warning. And a thank-you. She got me writing again. And while there's no guarantee that I will be able to assume a cooler, less emotional, more philosophical posture the next time my words are subject to review, I refuse to look that far down the line. At the moment it's more important that I feel comfortable.

# Political Positions

I am writing this from a squatting position. Cowering, actually. Inside a small closet in my home in Los Angeles. I spend an inordinate amount of time here these days. Eating. Sleeping. With an occasional reprieve for either a bathroom break or a conjugal visit with my wife, who is similarly hiding in another closet. Such is the result of being in Hollywood during a political season that makes any of the recent storms endured by Florida seem like sighs from an elderly aunt.

For me, politics began in a seated position. In dining rooms. Around seder and Thanksgiving tables where, as a young boy, I would listen in wonderment as relatives liberally employed the present tense when talking about FDR, who, at that point in time, had been quite dead for well over eighteen years. However, even my most polite suggestion about conjugating the verbs in deference to a previous generation were answered with shouts of "You're too young to understand!" Which I didn't. And still don't, because the vast majority of those very relatives are now just as dead as FDR and selfishly took all explanations to their graves with them.

In college, politics moved outdoors and, for the most part, I was standing. Shoulder to shoulder with dozens upon dozens of fellow sloganeers voicing outrage about Vietnam, Nixon, Agnew, and Kent State. Standing upright was the position from which we were best heard. It was also the best position to start running from the tear-gas canisters being fired in our direction. The decibels of my relatives had been replaced by the chemicals of the National Guard, and if I wanted to spare myself burning eyes and irritated flesh, getting a good running start was advisable.

After I enjoyed life for many years as an East Coast writer, a television show I'd created brought me out to Los Angeles. The promise was exciting. I remember walking off the plane looking forward to raising our young children away from the travails of New York winters. Little did I know that walk would be the last time I actually stood up in this town.

I should probably mention here that my politics are, by and large, left of center. Notice I said *my* politics. *My* opinions. *My* feelings about what is right and what is wrong with the world we live in and the course of action we might want to consider to indeed make things better. And while I can hold my own in a political discussion, I admit that I am not smart enough to write about it. Which suits me just fine, as I am not so passionate that I would feel the need to express myself even if I were smart enough to write about it. That I leave to others. All I ask, as a human being who is trying his utmost to get from one end of his life to the other—and perhaps leave his mark on some areas where his strengths *do* lie—is that my opinion be respected. Especially by those whose opinions are the same as mine.

That's my problem, however. I am not liberal enough for my liberal friends. Nor am I vocal enough for my exceptionally loud friends. Quiet dinners seem to be a thing of the past, as discussions are no longer the exchange of ideas so much as tests of resolve. My friends are shouting the way my relatives did at those FDR dinners. And all my attempts to stand are met by forces strong enough to drive me backward. And penniless. More times than not the candidate everyone's supporting is actually present at the home we're invited to, so checkbooks are required. Recently it cost my wife and me three thousand dollars to have dinner at a friend's house, and we still ended up stopping for something to eat on our way home. Invitations descend upon us like plagues. They are faxed to us. They arrive by mail on engraved stationery. And they are e-mailed by people who've embraced self-aggrandizing causes.

"Since when do you care so much about elephant poaching?" I asked a lifelong friend I thought I knew.

"Me? I don't give a shit about elephants."

"Then why are you hosting Kenya Awareness Night this Thursday?"

"Because this director I really want to do my movie is into it, so, you know."

"Jesus . . ."

All of our friends attended Kenya Awareness Night. We didn't. I happen to like elephants. But it was my father's seventy-seventh birthday. My father doesn't have strong feelings one way or another about elephants. He wishes them well, but he didn't necessarily want to spend his seventy-seventh birthday paying homage to them. So we took him to dinner at a local Italian restaurant, brought our nine-year-old daughter along with us, and returned home to a barrage of phone messages chiding us for not being there.

So now my oldest friend is angry because he feels that a seventy-seventh birthday isn't milestone enough to miss a pachyderm-fest. His ecologically sensitive wife is angry because the restaurant we took my dad to serves veal. My agent is mad because the Kenya Awareness Night party had a lot of people who could help me with a project I am currently trying to launch. His environmentally active wife is even angrier because we drove to the Italian restaurant in a car that wasn't a hybrid. And we just learned that my seventy-seven-year-old father is upset because our nine-year-old daughter didn't know who FDR was when he managed to bring his name up twenty-four times during his delicious birthday dinner.

It's come full circle. Make that full circle and then some. At least when I got shouted down at those seder and Thanksgiving tables I retreated to a seated position. But out here, in a town where social status is based on what people think everyone else's perception of you is, I've withdrawn. To my closet. Where I write in a squatting position. Where I plan on staying until the moving men come and load me into a van headed back to the East Coast. Where I can stretch my legs.

# The Queen and I

Not long ago, I wrote a television pilot for a network that shall remain unnamed. It was a family comedy about four generations living in the same house. The executives at the unnamed network liked the script so much they gave me the go-ahead to make the pilot. A budget was approved. A director and writing staff were hired. Sets were designed and built. Locations were scouted. A shooting date was set. And an audience of three hundred was invited.

But then, after we'd spent well over a million dollars on the project, I pulled the plug on it because of a disagreement with the unnamed president of the unnamed network. The issue was casting. He didn't want me to give any roles to anyone over the age of fifty. I politely reminded him that this was just a tad absurd given that unless the series was going to be about the most precocious Amish family that ever lived, the prospect of Great-Grandpa being forty-eight years old just didn't ring true to me. "Do the math!" I argued.

"Alan, our audience isn't that literal."

"So we're saying these characters had children when they were twelve?"

"Trust me. No one will notice."


Looking back, I think I would have lost a lot of money over the years if I'd bet on writing about life as it really is. I was one of the original writers for *Saturday Night Live,* and as a full-fledged member of the baby boom, I figured there'd always be a large, built-in audience for my work that would age at the same rate I did. I simply assumed that as our lives progressed to include marriage, children, home owning, receding hairlines, escalating belt sizes, more nocturnal trips to the bathroom, etc., whatever my friends and I were going through at any given moment would become a never-ending source of entertainment fodder.

But I was wrong. Mainly because I had no way of predicting that when I reached my early fifties, the executives I'd be dealing with—and dependent upon for my livelihood—would miraculously still be in their twenties. Some had been hired right out of school; others were the same people who'd been on the scene back in the 1970s but they'd obviously been working so hard they never took the time to age.

How did this happen? Why am I the only one in Hollywood who got older? Why doesn't anyone else remember Vietnam? Or Willie Mays? Or blue suede shoes?

Think I'm kidding? Then how else would you explain the following conversation that actually took place between me and an unnamed executive at an unnamed movie studio?

"Great script, Alan. We just have a few notes."

"Sure."

"Starting with the character of the wife."

"Eleanor."

"Yes. She seems rather serious and unsexy."

"Well, Eleanor Roosevelt *was* rather serious and unsexy."

"Fine, but if we want to get Queen Latifah to play this part, we might have to make a few minor adjustments."

"Queen Latifah?"

"Yeah, she's real hot since that movie she did with Steve Martin, and she's looking for her next project."

"Queen Latifah as Eleanor Roosevelt?"

"Wouldn't that be great?"

"No, it's absurd."

"Why?"

"Because Eleanor Roosevelt wasn't black."

"Why are you being so difficult?"

"I'm sorry. I'm just having a little trouble envisioning the star of *Barbershop 2* being married to Franklin Delano Roosevelt."

"She's an incredibly versatile actress, Alan. We're even thinking about having her and whoever plays Franklin do a big dance number."

"Excuse me?"

"Maybe a hip-hop thing in the White House or in front of Congress."

"But FDR had polio. He was in a wheelchair."

"We have a note about that, too."

I ultimately got fired from that job. The unnamed executive at the unnamed movie studio told my agent that I was out of touch with today's audiences.

Dedication

This book, *Modern Ethics,* could not have seen the light of day without the encouragement of Rabbi Nathan R. Rosenzweig, who served as a living inspiration for the values explored within the pages that follow. Even these words underestimate what he has given to this journey, which has been more than three years in the making.

When I first approached Rabbi Rosenzweig, the spiritual leader of our local synagogue, and told him of my desire to explore the moral choices confronting twenty-first-century man, he nodded, locked the door to his study, looked into my eyes, and asked me why I was doing this.

"What do you know?" he pleaded. "Who sent you?"

"No one sent me," I assured him. "I'm just doing research for a book."

"Swear."

"Swear?"

"To God."

"To God?"

"Who then?"

"I swear to God, Rabbi Rosenzweig."

"Good. Now, you see what I just did? I presented you with a modern ethical choice. Whether to think I was hiding something or give me the benefit of the doubt because I'm a rabbi who would never even think of embezzling from the temple's building fund."

He leaned back in his armchair and exhaled a prodigious sigh that only a man of God could muster. I had sought Rabbi Rosenzweig's counsel as he had written on this very subject himself in his novel *I Swear I Didn't Do It* (Shalom Press, 2002), which a starred *Kirkus* review said was "written with the uncanny authority of a man intimately familiar with the darkest recesses of the guilty mind. If one didn't know better, you'd say the rabbi himself was the protagonist and that this was not a work of fiction."

"So, how can I be of help?" he asked.

"Well, I plan on citing cases where different people had choices to make and what went into the making of their eventual decisions."

"What people?" he snapped as his back arched in what could best be described as clerical recoil. "Anyone local?"

"Well, if anyone local has a story to tell . . ."

"Because even a local person can do things out of character due to pressure to yield to the monetary demands of a recently widowed congregant threatening him with exposure after he took her to a desert spa for a weekend on a wrongheaded attempt to help her cope with the first step of the grieving process."

"Oh my . . ."

"What do you mean?"

"Nothing, Rabbi."

"Swear to God?"

"Who then?" I laughed. He didn't.

"So the man in this particular example," he continued, "a man with a wife and family of his own, mind you, had a choice to make. Does he risk losing everything dear to him, or does he first try to reason with the woman before resorting to covering his head with a prayer shawl to avoid detection when he goes out at night to slash the tires of her SUV?"

Oddly enough, I was familiar with the tire-slashing incident. We live in a small town in suburban New Jersey, and the boy who was charged (a troubled eleven-year-old who lost his father to the highly coincidental heart attack he suffered while buying jogging shorts) happens to live a few doors down from me.

"Steven Jogardnick."

"Who?" asked the rabbi.

"The kid who's under house arrest for slashing those tires."

"Oh, right," said the rabbi. "That fat little turd with the unsightly overbite."

"Fat little turd?"

"One of God's foul tips, don't you think?"

"But if Steven was wrongly accused . . ." I protested.

"I'd advise you to be mindful of your tone, young man. Remember the seventh commandment. About honoring thy rabbis."

"Excuse me, but the commandment says to honor thy father and thy mother. It says nothing about rabbis. And that's the fifth commandment, by the way. The seventh says one shall not commit adultery, which I believe the man in this particular example has already broken, along with the third, eighth, ninth, tenth, and very possibly the fourth if he committed any of the above on a Saturday."

"Your point?"

"That shouldn't a rabbi, with all due respect, be better familiar with the Ten Commandments than the one in this example seems to be?"

"Yes, I firmly believe that a rabbi should."

"Then why isn't this rabbi—"

"This is an unpredictable world we live in. And life doesn't always run along the direct course we chart to reach our goals. So if a young man dreams of becoming a rabbi but then his father dies so he has no choice but to take over his plumbing and heating business to support his aging mother, then he does what he has to do at that time. And if years later, after his mother passes on, he still has that burning desire to be in the rabbinate but has neither the time nor patience to learn the Hebrew language so he goes online and gets a clergyman's certificate, is he any less a man of God than someone who has graduated the Jewish Theological Seminary? I don't think so. Plus, given those circumstances, I truly think that the young man in the example has done quite admirably given that he is actually . . ."

"A plumber?" I asked with the same horrified intonation with which one would deliver the line "You mean to tell me that two of my sons were Bar Mitzvahed by a man who's better trained to lie on his back and scoop the sludge from a clogged sink?"

"Call that young man in this particular example what you wish," he responded. "That is your prerogative. Just know that not only do I disagree but I fully expect that anything we've discussed will not leave this room as it falls under . . ."

"Author-plumber confidentiality?"

And though I personally didn't subscribe to the validity of such a bond, I suddenly found myself with my own decision to make and the full understanding of its rather far-reaching implications. On the one hand, the reputations of an innocent boy and a slutty widow were at stake. On the other hand, the tranquillity of a faithful community would most definitely be upset by the news that the man who chants the prayers for their dead may not know a Torah from a sump pump. Sensitive to the fact that either choice could provide a most disastrous result, I wondered if there was a compromise to be discussed.

"Bargain?" he asked. "You want to bargain with a rabbi?"

"I'd love to," I answered. "But since there are no rabbis here at the moment, maybe you and I should take a crack at it."

"And just what are you proposing?"

"That I won't tell anyone you're a fraud if you confess to the tire-slashing incident."

"I can't do that," he responded. "Such an admission would destroy my credibility with the congregation."

"Then what if I don't tell anyone you're a fraud and if you return all the money you embezzled from the temple's building fund to pay off the slutty widow?"

"Can't do that either," he said, shaking his head. "That's a lot more money than I'll ever be able to pay back on my salary."

"Then what if I don't tell anyone you're a fraud and you give me the slutty widow's phone number?"

"You're out of your mind."

"Maybe so," I answered. "But that's my final offer."

"Don't do it," he insisted. "She'll destroy your life."

"Let me worry about the destruction of my life."

"I can't have this on my head."

"All of a sudden things are going to be on your head?" I asked. "Until this conversation absolutely nothing that was going on in your sordid life was anywhere near your head. So don't bullshit me, okay? Given all that I know about you, I'd say you're getting off rather easy."

"Yeah, but . . ."

"Come on, buddy. All I'm asking for is a simple seven-digit telephone number. Now cough it up."

"Make it six."

"Excuse me?"

"I'll tell you six of the digits. This way if I'm ever asked if I gave you her phone number, it won't be on my head when I say no."

"Again with your head?"

"Please."

"Fine. Just make sure that the six digits you give me are in the right order."

"Really?"

"Hey!"

"Okay, okay."

It was an encounter that could best be described as life-altering, as I got a new girlfriend and a new plumber and changed temples in the same afternoon. So it is for these reasons that this book is dedicated to Nathan R. Rosenzweig—if in fact that's his real name.

# Happy

*The vestibule of an apartment building. Nothing out of the ordinary: a door one enters from the street, a small area with a tenant directory on the wall, and another door that one has to either use a key or be buzzed by a tenant to open.*

*SL of the vestibule is a small lobby, with a few apartment doors and an elevator door on its perimeter.*

*Drab is the motif here. Chipped paint, faint vestiges of graffiti that defiantly still peeps through the efforts of a whitewash, and lighting a few watts dimmer than it really should be. The overall feeling is that although the place is clean and well maintained, it is probably part of a low-income housing development that years and lack of funds have gotten the better of.*

*The time is the present.*

*AT RISE: Donald Rappaport, forty-two, opens the outside door and enters the vestibule. He is wearing a suit and looks extremely hot, as his forehead is beading with perspiration and the underarms of his suit jacket are drenched with huge wet spots.*

*He scans the directory, finds the name he's looking for, tries to open the inside door, realizes it's locked, then pushes the button next to the name on the directory.*

*While waiting for a response, he tries to cool off by fanning himself with his attaché case.*

> DONALD

Fucking hot . . .

*He pushes the button again and while waiting for a response tries to cool off by fanning himself with his tie.*

> DONALD *(cont'd)*

So fucking hot.

*He pushes the button a third time and while waiting for a response tries to cool off by fanning himself by opening and closing the outside door a number of times.*

> DONALD *(cont'd)*

Fucking Florida.

*Through the intercom we hear the offstage voice of an older man.*

MAN'S VOICE

Yes?

DONALD

Mr. Haliday?

MAN'S VOICE

Who'd like to know?

DONALD

I would.

MAN'S VOICE

And you would be . . . ?

DONALD

From New York.

MAN'S VOICE

And you think that narrows it down?

DONALD

Oh, don't mind me. I'm just a little disori-
ented. You see, my parents live in Boca Raton
and I just flew here with my wife and kids because tonight's the first night of Passover.

MAN'S VOICE

And you think *that* narrows it down? This
time of year everyone from New York comes
to Florida.

DONALD
Well, I wouldn't say *everyone.*

MAN'S VOICE
Oh, that's right. John Gotti's still in jail.
Now, what can I do for you?

DONALD
Look, my name is Donald Rappaport, and
after we landed in West Palm Beach, I rented
a Ford Taurus and dropped everyone off at
my folks' place in Boca and then drove
straight here, on I-95, to Delray Beach to try
to find George Haliday because I want to
speak to him. Are you him?

MAN'S VOICE
I *could* be. But only on one condition.

DONALD
Which is?

MAN'S VOICE
That I don't have to hear one more word
about your itinerary. Deal?

DONALD
Deal.

MAN'S VOICE
Then yes, I *am* George Haliday.

DONALD

*The* George Haliday?

MAN'S VOICE

*A* George Haliday.

DONALD

But I'm looking for *the* George Haliday.

MAN'S VOICE

*The* George Haliday who's the superinten-
dent of this building?

DONALD

No, *the* George Haliday who used to play for
the Mets.

MAN'S VOICE

Oh, that *the* George Haliday.

DONALD

Yes, that *the* George Haliday. Are you him?

MAN'S VOICE

I was.

DONALD

Well, that makes no sense.

MAN'S VOICE

How come?

DONALD

Because either you're *the* George Haliday
who used to play for the Mets or you're not.
It's not like you used to play for the Mets but
you no longer used to play for them. You either did or you didn't, so you either are or
you aren't.

MAN'S VOICE

Ow!

DONALD

Something wrong?

MAN'S VOICE

Yeah, I just threw my back out trying to follow that speech.

DONALD

Sorry.

MAN'S VOICE

May I remind you, sir, that I am a janitor.
Break something, I'll fix it. Soil it, I'll clean it.
Lose it, I'll replace it. Anything more compli-
cated, I have to call somebody. Please don't
make me have to do that with this conversation.

DONALD

Okay. All I want to know is . . .

> MAN'S VOICE
>
> ... if I'm the George Haliday who once played baseball.

> DONALD
>
> Yes.

> MAN'S VOICE
>
> Yes.

> DONALD
>
> You are?

> MAN'S VOICE
>
> Yes.

> DONALD
>
> You're Happy Haliday?

> MAN'S VOICE
>
> I'm Happy Haliday.

> DONALD
>
> Great!

> MAN'S VOICE
>
> Now, is there something you'd like to talk to me about?

> DONALD
>
> Yes, very much.

MAN'S VOICE

And you would like to have this talk face-to-face?

DONALD

Yes, I would.

MAN'S VOICE

So then I'll buzz you in, okay?

DONALD

Okay.

MAN'S VOICE

See how simple life can be if you just get to the point?

*The buzzer sounds. Donald pushes open the door, enters the inner lobby, and approaches the door on the SL wall. He waits patiently for it to open. While he does, he fixes his hair and collar as if he was primping for an important meeting.*

*The door opens and George "Happy" Haliday appears. He is a sixty-four-year-old black man with gray hair, eyeglasses, and an infectious smile.*

HAPPY

George Haliday.

DONALD

Donald Rappaport.

*They shake hands.*

HAPPY

Well, it's nice to finally have a face to go along with the voice.

*Donald just stands there, as if mesmerized.*

HAPPY *(cont'd)*

You okay?

*Donald is in awe.*

HAPPY *(cont'd)*

Will you be talking soon?

DONALD

Oh, sorry. I guess I'm just a little starstruck.

*Happy looks around at the setting, taking in the mundane dinginess of it all.*

> HAPPY
>
> Well, I can see how all this might be overwhelming. But don't worry. I think you'll find that we janitors are just like ordinary people—once you get past all the glitter and the goddamn paparazzi. So . . . Donald . . . *Qué pasa?*

> DONALD
>
> I used to watch you play.

> HAPPY
>
> Oh, yeah?

> DONALD
>
> Yeah. My dad worked in the city. . . . I'm originally from Long Island. There's a shocker, huh?

> HAPPY
>
> I didn't say a word. But now that you mention it . . .

> DONALD
> *(bracing himself)*
>
> You're going to make fun of me now, aren't you?

HAPPY

No. Maybe later. So, you were telling me about your dad.

DONALD

All I was saying is that lots of times I would go to work with him on the weekends and afterward we'd drive up to the Polo Grounds and I'd see you play. I was eight.

HAPPY

Polo Grounds ain't there no more, huh?

DONALD

The city knocked it down and put up apartment buildings a few years after the Mets moved into Shea.

HAPPY

And is that how you found out where I lived? From the Mets?

DONALD

No. I learned you were down here from that article I read about you.

HAPPY

What article?

DONALD

In the *New York Post*. That series you were in?

HAPPY

Series?

DONALD

Oh . . .

HAPPY

What kind of series?

DONALD

Well . . .

HAPPY

Go ahead. Tell me.

DONALD

. . . The *New York Post,* in their sports section, has a feature called "What Might've
Been." And, about a month ago, they had a
piece . . .

HAPPY

About me?

DONALD

I'm sorry. From the way it was written, I just
assumed that they spoke to you. . . .

HAPPY

What'd they have? A lot of that next Willie
Mays stuff?

DONALD
Yeah.

HAPPY
Look, would you like to come in? Tenants
catch me chatting like this, they'll think I got
too much free time on my hands and give me
more stuff to do.

DONALD
Sure.

*Happy indicates the inside of his apartment. Donald enters,
and Happy closes the door behind them—revealing that he is
walking with the aid of a cane.*

HAPPY
Would you like something to eat?

DONALD
Yeah, I'll have a slice of apple pie, heated up,
and a large milk.

HAPPY
Now would that be regular milk or two per-
cent?

DONALD
You have both? Wow.
                    *(off Happy's look)*
On second thought I'm going to have a big
dinner later—you know, at the seder. So
maybe I shouldn't spoil my appetite.

HAPPY

Damn, and here I was so looking forward to cooking for you. So, what are we talking about?

*Donald opens his attaché case and takes out a clear plastic cube that has a baseball covered with signatures inside.*

DONALD

Here. Check this out.

*He hands the cube to Happy.*

HAPPY

Wow . . .

DONALD

The 1962 team. Pretty amazing, huh?

HAPPY

No pun intended.

DONALD

Oh. No. Although that *was* the year they started calling you guys the Amazin' Mets, right?

HAPPY

Right. Our amazing team that lost 120 games, which I believe is still the record for the most losses in one season by any major-league team in baseball history.

DONALD
Yeah, it still is.


HAPPY
Look at the names. Casey, there's Gil
Hodges, Elio Chacon . . .


DONALD
Yeah, my grandmother got really excited
when she first heard Elio Chacon's name because she thought he was Jewish.

*Happy stares at him.*


DONALD *(cont'd)*
She thought it was Eliosha Cohen.

*Happy continues to stare.*


DONALD *(cont'd)*
True story.

*Happy continues to stare.*


DONALD *(cont'd)*
Now you're going to make fun of me?


HAPPY
No, not yet.
*(re: the ball)*
Say, is it okay if I take this out of the cube?

DONALD
Are your hands clean?

HAPPY
Excuse me?

*Donald grabs Happy's hands and examines them.*

HAPPY *(cont'd)*
Look, I just want to see it, not perform
surgery on it.

DONALD
Yeah, I guess they're all right.

HAPPY
I'm flattered.

*Donald takes the ball out of the cube and hands it to Happy.*

DONALD
But try to hold it by the seams.

HAPPY
Are you always so annoying?

DONALD
Pretty much.

HAPPY
So, where'd you get this ball?

DONALD

My dad. . . . Like I said, we used to go to the games all the time. He'd been a New York Giants fan, you know, before they moved to San Francisco. So when the National League came back to the city, well, it didn't matter that the Mets stunk. In fact, that was part of the charm. I'd sit there and see the players letting ground balls go through their legs, and tripping over their feet when they were rounding bases, and I'd look at my dad and say, "I can do that," and he'd look back at me and say, "I believe you can," and we'd laugh about that all the way home.

*Donald laughs at the memory.*

HAPPY

So, where'd you get this ball?

DONALD

You see, the Yankees were too good. They were exciting. But there was no way an average kid like me could ever actually relate to those guys. But you . . .

*Again Donald shakes his head and savors the laugh.*

HAPPY

Ball? Get? Where?

DONALD

Well, look who's being annoying now! And where's my pie? I got this ball the first day you played for the Mets.

HAPPY

Really?

DONALD

They'd just brought you up. On September first. The day the teams can expand their rosters for the final pennant drive, right?

HAPPY

*(smiling)*

Yeah. There I was, sitting in some Howard Johnson's down in Tidewater, when they call me with the news that I'm going up—for the pennant drive to a team that was fifty-seven games out of first place with only twenty-eight left to play—and it was the greatest day of my life. They gave me a plane ticket, I called my folks, and when I landed in New York and stepped up to that plate for the first time, I was . . .

DONALD

Happy.

HAPPY

Happy. I grew up across the street from the Polo Grounds. Used to watch Willie Mays do what he did from our kitchen window. So now here I am, playing his old position, hitting those two home runs, and I'm . . .

DONALD

Happy.

HAPPY

Happy. And that's what I told those sportswriters and that's how that whole Happy Haliday business got started. All those banners, those pins, that billboard near the Holland Tunnel . . .

DONALD

That's also when my dad started calling me that.

HAPPY

Happy?

DONALD

Uh-huh.

HAPPY

Happy Rappaport?

DONALD

Well, I'll admit it didn't have the same ring to it that Happy Haliday did, but dads don't usually say the last name when they're calling their kids so it worked out okay. . . . This ball? The second time you were up?

HAPPY

The single?

DONALD

The pitch before it.

HAPPY

The foul ball?

DONALD

This is it.

HAPPY

That's the ball?

DONALD

Yep. We were sitting in the second level, behind the plate, and this ball came screaming back at us. I brought my glove to the game, but there was no way I was going to catch this thing without it ripping my entire arm off my body. So my dad just nonchalantly reached over, stuck his huge meat hook of a hand in front of me, snagged the ball out of the air, and said, "Here you go." And here we are. It's thirty-five years later, and this is still the closest I've ever come to catching a foul ball at a game.

### HAPPY

And what about those signatures? I don't remember swinging at any balls that had all
those names on it.

### DONALD

Those I got on the last day of that season.
Someone who worked for my dad had a
friend who got us passes to the clubhouse.
So I brought this ball so I could get your
autograph after the game. I ended up getting
everybody's except yours. We waited for
you, but . . . you never came back from
the hospital. So we went home and just figured we'd get your autograph the following
season.

### HAPPY

Sorry. Imagine how *I* felt, though. I get hit by
a pitch, run to first, steal second, steal third,
score on a sacrifice fly, collapse in the dugout,
get taken to Lenox Hill for "precautionary"
X-rays, and the next thing I know they're
drilling holes in my skull because I had blood
clots. Before that day, I'd never even heard of
blood clots; but now I had some and they
were going to keep me from doing the only
thing I ever cared about doing.

### DONALD

I wrote to you that winter.

HAPPY

A lot of people sent cards, get-well
wishes. . . . At one point they were actually
delivering mail that was just addressed to
"Happy, New York City."

DONALD

That was me.

HAPPY

You sent those?

DONALD

Yeah. My father said you needed your rest,
so I just wrote "Happy, New York City" on
the envelope and put a blank sheet of paper
inside because I didn't want to tire you out by
making you read too many words.

HAPPY

I appreciated it. Your father still call you
"Happy" after it was all over for me?

DONALD

Yeah.

HAPPY

Really?

DONALD

A lot. He always pointed to you as an example of how a person should enjoy life in the

moment because you never know what's waiting around the corner.

> HAPPY

You mean, sort of like a "Man makes plans and God laughs" kind of thing?

> DONALD

No, I'd say more along the lines of "Be careful what you wish for because you might get it."

> HAPPY

Why?

> DONALD

Because you got hit in the head with a ninety-mile-an-hour fastball.

> HAPPY

I didn't wish for that.

> DONALD

Yeah, but . . . you didn't?

> HAPPY

Who would wish for a thing like that?

> DONALD

I see. So maybe it was more in the "smile is a frown turned upside down" area.

                    HAPPY
That must've been it.

*Donald looks at his watch.*

                    HAPPY *(cont'd)*
Late for something?

                    DONALD
Huh?

                    HAPPY
You keep looking at your watch.

                    DONALD
Oh, just a habit.

                    HAPPY
What time's your seder?

                    DONALD
Sundown.

                    HAPPY
And what time is sundown?

                    DONALD
Whatever time that everybody's hungry. It's a
Jewish thing. Look, would you mind signing
that ball?

> HAPPY
> *(surprised)*
> You want my autograph?

> DONALD
> Yeah.

> HAPPY
> You sure? I can't remember the last time someone asked me to sign something that didn't have an invoice number on it.

> DONALD
> You're the only name that's missing on it, and it would mean a lot.

> HAPPY
> If you say so.

*Donald reaches into his jacket pocket, pulls out a fancy pen, and hands it to Happy.*

> HAPPY *(cont'd)*
> How should I do this?

> DONALD
> Well, you just find an open spot on the ball and sign your name there.

> HAPPY
> I mean the pen. Where's the point on this thing?

> DONALD

Oh.

> *(showing him)*

You just twist the top and . . . there you go.

> HAPPY

And what about this shit over here?

> DONALD

What shit?

> HAPPY

This rubber shit.

*Happy shows him the pen.*

> DONALD

Oh, that's just padding to rest your fingers on while you're writing.

*Happy stares at him.*

> DONALD *(cont'd)*

It's really comfortable.

*Happy continues to stare.*

> DONALD *(cont'd)*

It was a gift.

*Happy continues to stare.*

                    DONALD *(cont'd)*
You're going to make fun of me now?


                        HAPPY
                      *(nodding)*
You've given me no choice.


                        DONALD
Go ahead.


                        HAPPY
Ready?


                        DONALD
                  *(bracing himself)*
Yes.


                        HAPPY
You're a Sissy Mary.


                        DONALD
. . . That's it?


                        HAPPY
That's it.


                        DONALD
Well, you nailed my fat ass on that one. So,
now that that's over with . . .
                  *(indicating ball)*
. . . if you don't mind.

HAPPY

Oh. Boy, I'm really honored.

*He spins the ball in his hand, looking for a place to sign.*

DONALD

There's a spot.

HAPPY

Where?

DONALD

Between Marv Throneberry and Choo Choo
Coleman.

HAPPY

Little tight, don't you think?

DONALD

Not really.

HAPPY

Oh, here we go. Now, should it be "To Donald" or "Don" or one of your kids?

DONALD

No, no, no. Just your name.

HAPPY

But . . .

DONALD

It shouldn't be "to" anyone.


HAPPY

But you flew down, you landed in West Palm Beach, you drove the rented Taurus to my house. I feel like I should say something special.


DONALD

I appreciate that, but it's much more valuable if it's not personalized to anyone.


HAPPY

What do you mean by "more valuable"?


DONALD

It's worth more.


HAPPY

To who?


DONALD

To a buyer.


HAPPY

Excuse me?


DONALD

Well, if a collector is in the market for something like this, he's more apt to pay top dollar if it just has the athlete's name on it—as opposed to something that's made out to a specific person, because when he goes to sell it, *his* buyer might not want a ball that's made out to someone else.

> HAPPY
> *(suspicious)*
> You know, we both know what it is that I do for a living, but I don't believe we ever got around to talking about what you do. Would you mind it much if I ask what line of work you happen to be in, Mr. Rappaport?

> DONALD
> I deal in sports memorabilia.

> HAPPY
> And what exactly does that mean?

> DONALD
> It means that I go to shows—baseball-card shows, sports conventions, auctions—and buy mementoes from other dealers that I then try to sell to collectors who come into one of my stores, or sometimes I sell them privately.

*He hands Happy a business card.*

> HAPPY
> *(reading)*
> "The Sports Kingdom."

DONALD

I have four stores in the tri-state area.

HAPPY

So let me see if I understand this correctly. This ball with all these autographs on it is worth money.

DONALD

Yes.

HAPPY

And if I write my autograph on it . . .

DONALD

It will be worth more money.

HAPPY

Why?

DONALD

There'd be no other ball like it. That original team. Three of them Hall of Famers—based on the careers they had with other teams before they came to the Mets, mind you. But still, they're dead, so they can never sign another ball ever again, and the rest of these players are probably scattered all over the country and it would take a fortune to go track them down.

HAPPY

So how much could you get?

DONALD

For that ball?

HAPPY

Approximately.

DONALD

I can tell you exactly.

HAPPY

So tell me exactly.

DONALD

Twenty-eight thousand.

HAPPY

Dollars?

DONALD

That's right.

HAPPY

So let me see if I understand this correctly. You actually think that you can take this ball and sell it for exactly—

DONALD

I *know* I can sell that ball for exactly twenty-eight thousand dollars.

HAPPY

And how's that?

                              DONALD
It's already sold.

                              HAPPY
It is?

                              DONALD
Yes. Once you sign it, that is.

                              HAPPY
And, just so I know, how did that happen?

                              DONALD
I know a man up in New Jersey whose name
is Joe Eastern, and he's a collector, and he
called me. You see, Happy, there's so much
memorabilia out there, the market is so
flooded, that many collectors like to special-
ize in just one particular category that they
have a passion for. The 1961 Yankees is a big
attraction. Anything to do with Muhammad
Ali, some of the great Boston Celtic teams,
you know . . . and this guy . . .

                              HAPPY
Joe Eastern.

                              DONALD
That's right. Joe Eastern . . .

                              HAPPY
He the one who gave you this Sissy Mary pen
as a gift?

DONALD

No, but he did tell me that he grew up on
Long Island and that he was eleven years old
when the Mets came into existence and I told
him I had a ball in mint condition with the
original team's signatures on it with the exception of yours, and he said if you signed
it . . . well, I negotiated a price of twenty-
eight thousand dollars.

HAPPY

So you're going to part with this ball.

DONALD

Yes.

HAPPY

*(sarcastic)*

This ball that's filled with all those happy
memories of when your hero dad caught it
and saved that cute little baby face of yours
from being scrambled.

DONALD

Well, yeah. . . .

HAPPY

*(raising his voice)*

That same father who called you Happy.
After me, by the way. Who the hell are you,
Mr. Rappaport? I played baseball because I
loved it. I still love it. Every year I stop by

those spring-training camps when the teams are down here—they don't know me from a hole in the ground. To them I'm just another fan, and they're right. I am a fan. And you told me that you were one, too. But now I see that all you really came here for was to get an old man's signature on this ball so you can sell memories for a profit.

DONALD

Happy . . .

HAPPY

No. Mr. Rappaport! You're not a fan!

DONALD

Happy . . .

HAPPY

You're a scavenger!

DONALD

Happy!

HAPPY

What!

DONALD

I came here to give *you* this ball.

HAPPY

Excuse me? Would you mind indulging an old man by repeating that last sentence one more time? Just in case my heart stops and I die.


DONALD

Joe Eastern offered me twenty-five thousand dollars for the ball. But I insisted on exactly twenty-eight—which is exactly one thousand dollars for every game you played in the major leagues. It's not a lot by today's standards, but I just thought there was a certain ring to the way it sounded.


HAPPY

So let me see if I understand this correctly. I sign this ball . . .


DONALD

And Joe Eastern owes you twenty-eight thousand dollars.


HAPPY

I just shamed you into this, didn't I?


DONALD

No . . .


HAPPY

Me calling you a scavenger and all.


DONALD

No . . .

> HAPPY

And this isn't one of those Jewish guilt things
I keep hearing about.

> DONALD

No.

> HAPPY

So right from the time you buzzed my button
you were going to do this?

> DONALD

Yeah.

> HAPPY

No. Something's wrong with this story.

> DONALD

Why do you say that?

> HAPPY

It doesn't add up.

> DONALD

What doesn't add up?

> HAPPY

You know, I've tried my best all these years
not to be bitter. That doesn't do anyone any
good. One newspaper guy once figured out
that if I'd kept up those numbers I had, you

know, over the length of a normal career, I'd
be in the Hall of Fame. Well, that kind of talk
don't do anyone any good either. Sure, it
would have been great if I was Happy Holiday for longer than I was. But I wasn't. So I
try my best not to mourn for the life I didn't
have. And I think I'm doing an okay job. We
raised five kids in this place, my wife and I.
She worked, I worked, and somehow we
managed to send five happy people out into
this world. But now you come here offering
me this incredible generosity—Jesus, more
money than I've ever seen in any one place at
any one time—and one part of me wants to
cry and another part is suspicious and says
that this doesn't add up. That there's a lie
here that hasn't been said yet.


                    DONALD
There's no lie, Happy. Here. Here's Joe Eastern's phone number. Call him and see for
yourself that . . .


                    HAPPY
No, no. I believe that part.


                    DONALD
Then what part don't you believe? The Taurus? I swear to you I rented a Ford Taurus.
I'm not proud of it. But look outside, it's
right by the curb.

HAPPY
*(shaking his head)*

It's the pacing. The constant looking at your watch, I've seen executive types before. Suits, tiny phones that make them look like they're talking into their hands. Guys who are here but on their way to there. Are there but have to cut it short because they're already late somewhere else. Basically we're talking about guys who are never where they want to be. So now I look at you and do my best to figure out where you're supposed to be instead of here. Can you tell me that? Where you *really* should be right now.

DONALD

In Boca.

HAPPY

With your family.

DONALD

Yeah.

HAPPY

But instead you came down here. You read an article, flew down, and drove a rented Taurus to Delray Beach so you can give someone you never met a twenty-eight-thousand-dollar baseball an hour before the start of a holiday dinner, when you're going to be here in Florida for how long?

DONALD
Seven days.

HAPPY
Seven days. Is that how long Passover lasts?

DONALD
That's how long shiva lasts.

HAPPY
The shiva?

DONALD
The mourning period. My father died last night. We flew down here for his funeral.

HAPPY
*(sympathetic)*
There's more, right?

DONALD
We hadn't spoken in years. We had a fight and I got real pissed at him and he got real pissed at me and we were both acting like we were going to live forever and had all the time in the world to make up with each other.

HAPPY
What was the fight about?

DONALD
We both forgot. But we were both stubborn. My mom tried to intervene. My sisters, my

brother . . . All I know is that I was starting to miss him and then, about a month ago, that article about you was in the *New York Post* and I sent it to my dad with a note attached to it that said, "Remember?" And a few days later I got a package in the mail. A box. Inside of it was this ball, and a note that said, "Yes, I remember." I called him and we stayed on the phone for over three hours and at the end of the conversation decided that we would give you this ball together—when I came down for Passover. Then around three o'clock this morning my mom phoned. He had a heart attack.

                    HAPPY
Had you two spoken since that three-hour call?

                    DONALD
                    *(smiling)*
Every night.

                    HAPPY
                    *(smiling)*
No shit?

                    DONALD
                    *(smiling)*
No shit.

HAPPY

So I did good?

DONALD

You did real good. Thanks.

*A beat. Donald checks his watch.*

DONALD *(cont'd)*

Look, I should be getting back to my parents' house. Here's Joe Eastern's number. After you sign the ball, why not give him a buzz and you can work out all the details with him directly.

HAPPY

Well, I'm not sure I want to do that.

DONALD

Oh, would you like me to call him for you?

HAPPY

No. I'm just not so sure that I want to sell this thing so fast.

DONALD

Happy . . .

HAPPY

I know, I know—there's a lot anyone can do with twenty-eight thousand dollars. But just

like you have your quirky ways about you, I
was brought up to feel that a man should not
accept any gift that he himself could not af-
ford to have given.

DONALD

Don't let false pride enter this, Happy. Because I don't know exactly how much it was
worth your getting me and my dad back together again. As far as I'm concerned, I'm the
one who got the bargain. But the decision is
yours. There's the ball. And there's the phone
number. Take care, Happy Haliday.

HAPPY

You too, Happy Rappaport.

*Donald picks up his attaché case and turns to leave.*

DONALD

Bye.

HAPPY

Hey, Donald?

DONALD

Yeah?

HAPPY

Thank you.

DONALD

Sure.

*Donald exits the apartment, crosses the lobby, and opens the door to the vestibule.*

> HAPPY
> *(through intercom)*
>
> And, Donald?

> DONALD
>
> Yeah?

> HAPPY
> *(through intercom)*
>
> Next Passover? If you and your family should decide to fly down to Florida?

> DONALD
>
> Yeah?

> HAPPY
> *(through intercom)*
>
> I'd really love it if you had the seder here, in my apartment.

> DONALD
>
> Really?

> HAPPY
> *(through intercom)*
>
> Yeah. That way I could get to cook that big meal for you we were talking about earlier.

> DONALD
>
> And pie?

HAPPY
*(through intercom)*
Yes, pie.

DONALD
À la mode?

HAPPY
*(through intercom)*
Don't push it.

*Donald exits the building.*

*LIGHTS SLOWLY FADE OUT.*

# The Big Forgery

I believe in connections. The kinds that forever bind through shared experiences, secrets, or songs. I particularly like the connections, however subtle, that keep people united even after one of them has passed away—because they tend to keep the person alive that much longer. Like my maternal grandfather, who lived the often-heard saga of a refugee who emigrated from Europe on May 12, 1912. A confused, Yiddish-speaking boy arriving via ship and processed at Ellis Island, he worked in a sweatshop to help bring money into the apartment where he lived with his parents and eight brothers and sisters. As a result, his childhood was denied along with any semblance of a formal education. Still, he did his best to blend in by teaching himself the new language and by picking up as many colloquialisms as he possibly could along the way—so by the time he became my grandfather, to me the only detectable trace of his not having been born in America was the accent that all grandparents seemed to have back then. But I understood everything he said. His jokes. His stories about the Old Country. And he made me laugh. Hard. Real hard. One time so hard that I inadvertently, and quite audibly, broke wind. Which made me laugh even harder—all the while *he* kept laughing and repeating, "Alan made a forgery. Alan made a forgery."

Now, as a four-year-old boy who was just learning English himself, I had no reason to think that that wasn't what it was called. No reason to even consider that the one word my self-educated grandfather didn't fully get the hang of was the one that distinguishes the act of falsely creating, altering, or imitating a document or signature with intent to defraud from the noise a person makes when he's eaten too much cabbage. So, as far as I was concerned, that noise was called a forgery—and long after I'd learned its true meaning, the word *forgery* never failed to make me laugh hysterically while drawing befuddled stares from all who witnessed my outbursts. Like the dozens of moms and dads in that auditorium during a fifth-grade spelling bee. And the proctor in the room where I was taking the vocabulary portion of the SATs. And most recently, the judge, attorneys, and my fellow prospective jurors for the trial of a man accused of signing his name to elderly people's Social Security checks. Boy, did that make me laugh. Hard. Real hard. So hard that I, yes, so hard that I, a fifty-four-year-old man in a court of law, committed a forgery of my own. A rather explosive, window-rattling forgery that brought the proceedings to a dramatic halt as it came this close to tipping the scales of justice at an angle they had never assumed before. Everyone in the jury box, everyone in the entire courtroom for that matter, stopped what they were doing and took notice of my first laugh-induced forgery in a half-century. Even the judge, a burly cross between Oliver Wendell Holmes and Oliver Hardy, looked up from whatever documents he was perusing and simply said, "Wow."

I wasn't selected. The prosecutor dismissed me summarily, and the defense offered no argument otherwise. Whether it was due to my background, or my political leanings, or the hesitance of those impaneled to be in an enclosed space with me during deliberations is anybody's guess. But the time I'd spent there was invaluable, as jury selection is a feature of our democracy that I had never experienced firsthand before, and it served to keep me connected, albeit in a most unorthodox way, to a loving man I still think about whenever I laugh.

## Notes from a Western State

6:15 A.M. PST . . . A call from a sister in Nyack, New York, crying, "Turn on the news" . . . One plane, then another . . . One
tower . . . Jesus Christ, there goes the other. . . . They also got
the Pentagon? Probably going after the obvious targets like the
Sears Tower, Hoover Dam . . . Wracking my brain trying to figure out what in L.A. is worth hitting . . . Phone calls crisscross-
ing the country. "Did you get through? Is he okay? Did you
actually speak to him and he personally told you that he's
okay?" . . . Got to get back to my city. Yeah, yeah, I've been out
here for years but . . . Boy, is Gary Condit one lucky son of a
bitch or what? . . . Wayne St. Clare. Where did that name come
from? . . . Sang all the verses to "America the Beautiful" during
Yom Kippur services. It took about an hour. . . . A store put me
on a waiting list for a flag. . . . There's that name again. Who the
hell is Wayne St. Clare? . . . Went to a party Saturday night. People sad beyond authenticity. Hollywood grief-chic . . . Jesus, I
haven't thought about Wayne St. Clare since June 1972. Just out

of college. Employment agencies. Job hunting. Any job. Psych Degree—I know, I know, that's why I said any job. Adderson Business Memos. One World Trade Center. Brand-new. Smells of sawdust. Sheetrock. Finishing touches. Met with Wayne St. Clare. President of Larson's Business Memos. My dad's age. Everyone's dad's age. Loved business memos. Loved Tower One. Called it "my building" . . . Training for the NYC Marathon. Listening to oldies while I run. The song "Candy Man" reminds me of Wayne St. Clare, who, when he fired me for writing jokes on his time and on his business memos, did so by yelling, "Young man, leave my building now!" . . . November 2001. Flying to New York. On the plane I wonder if I would've had the balls to fight with hijackers like those others guys did. . . . JFK cabbie asks me what I do. I tell him that I write. He asks what I've written. I mention my last movie. He says he could've done a better job. . . . Check in to Essex House. 5:30 P.M. Starting to get dark. Maybe I should wait until the morning. No, I can't. Hop on a subway and head downtown. I look around and want to apologize to everyone for not being here when it happened. For not looking like they do as we approach the station at Broadway and Nassau Street. For consciously trying to not look like a tourist in a place I still consider home . . . Up onto the street. The smell. I'd wondered if it was still there or would I have to work extra hard to try to detect something. . . . Is this ghoulish? To experience the same thrill a child gets upon seeing in person a toy he only knows from television? What possible reason could I have to . . . My God. Ground Zero. Look what those assholes did to our city. To all those people. To Wayne St. Clare's building. A woman standing next to me started crying about the same time that I did. We hugged. . . . Later. On my laptop. Checked that "Portraits of Grief" section in the *Times*. No one named St. Clare . . . The night before the marathon. I wear an FDNY cap to a prerace pasta dinner in the park. The fat woman dishing out the food smiles, gives me extra rolls, and whispers seductively, "Take from this pot. It's fresher." . . . November 4. 6:00 A.M. On a bus to Staten Island. Lived in New York the first thirty-six years of my life, this is my first trip to Staten Island. . . . Mayor Giuliani tells us we're heroes, that guy who sang "God Bless America" during the World Series games leads us in song, a cannon goes off, and thirty thousand people say, "Fuck you, bin Laden" without uttering a word. . . . Halfway across the Verrazano, sixty thousand eyes look to the left and see the skyline. This time some people actually speak the words "Fuck you, bin Laden." . . . Brooklyn. Another first for me when a Hassidic woman gives me a high five as I run past her and her seventy-two children. . . . Queens. As I trudge up the slight gradient of the Fifty-ninth Street bridge, I hum the lyrics to the Paul Simon song about this very structure ("Slow down, you move too fast") and can't help but think that moving too fast is hardly my problem. . . . Manhattan. I wonder if any of these thousands cheering along First Avenue have any idea that I peed in my running shorts, just a little. . . . The Bronx. A guy on

crutches passes me. I'm starting to think about upping my pace. . . . Manhattan again. It's getting dark as I enter the park. I see a cop on a horse and wonder if it'd be considered a bribe if I offered him ten bucks for the horse. . . . Tavern on the Green. I throw my arms up into the air as I cross the finish line and find out that I came in 22,373rd place. Which means that, all told, I ran behind 22,372 asses. Still another first . . . What a day. Triumphant. Defiant . . . Monday morning. On my way back to JFK I play a hunch and dial information. There's a Larson's Business Memos at an uptown address. A guy named Steve St. Clare tells me they relocated two years ago despite the wishes of his father, who didn't want to leave "his building." Wayne St. Clare died at the age of eighty-one on September 7, and I still feel that was a good thing.

# Barbarians at the Plate

I'm a writer. I deal in words. When words are obvious, my job is easy. But during those inexplicable periods when my vocabulary betrays me, I just sit here, idiot dumb, unable to place words in any order due to the fact I no longer *know* any words. And if I *don't* write, my family starves. This is worrisome. My wife and children are good people who deserve a better fate. So the pressure is enormous. Last January, I found myself immersed in just this kind of pressure when the phone rang.

—Hello?

—Hi, is this Alan?

—Yes.

—Hi, Alan. This is Normie Wax.

—Who?

—Normie Wax. From the league.

—Normie Wax from *what* league?

—You know, our kids' Little League.

—Oh, yeah. Of course. How you doin', Normie?

—So you know me.

—No.

—Sure you do.

—I do?

—You saw me at all of the games last season.

—I did?

—Sure, I'm president of the league.

I did seem to remember one goofy guy who always walked around wearing a cap that said PREZ. The kind of cap that a grown-up named Normie Wax would, in fact, wear.

—Are you the guy with the hat?

—Yep, that's me.

—Uh-huh.

—My boy got me that hat.

—It's a beauty.

—Listen, Alan, the reason I'm calling is, I want to know if you'd consider becoming commissioner of our league.

—You're kidding.

—Well, I see you down at the field all the time working with your boy. So, the guys on the board and I thought you might be a good choice for commissioner.

—Well, first of all, let me say that I'm real flattered, Normie.

—You're welcome . . .

—But I do have one small question.

—Fire away, amigo.

—Well, what exactly does the commissioner do?

—Not much. It's mostly administrative. You'd make the schedule for the coming season, help launch the fund-raiser, preside over the major-league draft . . .

—Draft?

—Yeah. This weekend we'll hold tryouts, and the managers will rate the kids on how well they catch, throw, hit . . .

—Uh-huh.

—Hit for average, power, bat speed . . .

—Right.

—Bunting, stealing, how fast they run from home to first . . .

—Jesus, Normie.

—From first to second, second to third, third to home . . .

—My God, Normie . . .

—And how well they can turn a double play. Then on Monday night the managers will get together and draft the kids until their rosters are filled.

I'd been to some of those tryouts, and I'd seen those managers sitting on the sidelines feverishly feeding information about prepubescent kids into their laptop computers. They take this stuff quite seriously. In their own special way, they each looked like my accountant during tax season.

—Dad?

—Hey, kiddo.

—Who was that on the phone?

—The president of your Little League.

—The guy with the hat?

—Yeah, he asked if I wanted to be commissioner.

—Really?

—Yeah.

—Wow! Are you going to do it?

—I said I'd call him back. What do you think? Should I?

—Why not? I think it'd be fun.

Diversion plays a big role in a writer's life. It is what he seeks when he either can't—or doesn't want to—write. God knows, I wanted to write. I had an idea for a movie. A movie about a guy.

But with no words at my disposal, I was at a loss in describing who the guy was, what he said, whom he said it to, what other people said back to him, where anyone lived, and what happened to all of them. So I figured, why not pay heed to the request of my soon-to-be-very-gaunt son and grant his last wish by becoming commissioner of his Little League?

## TRYOUTS

—Hey, Normie.

—What do you say, Commish? Checking out this year's crop?

—Yeah. Some of these kids look pretty good. I like number 921 . . .

—He'll be on the Tigers.

—Number 1046 . . .

—The Orioles.

—And number 1173.

—Phillies.

—Wait a second, Normie. How do you know what teams these kids are going to be on two days before the draft?

—Well, if a kid is the son of an assistant coach, then he's on his dad's team automatically and doesn't have to go through the draft.

—Is that why I see all those managers swooping down on the parents after a kid has a good tryout?

—These guys *do* tend to get somewhat competitive.

Last year, after my son tried out, a number of coaches asked if I wanted to be their assistant. Some called the house. Others offered to buy me lunch. I just figured that was because they liked me and had a high regard for my baseball acumen. Little did I know that had I played my cards right, today I might be wearing a better watch.

## THE DRAFT

—Normie, this is amazing.

—What do you mean?

—The computer readouts, the doctors' reports, the lineage charts, the huddled conferences, the trading, the debating. I never knew any of this stuff went on.

—Always has.

—Geez.

—Well, only for the first three rounds or so. Until all the better players are taken. After that, it's pretty much of a toss-up, so things will go a lot quicker.

—Then what's the deal with Billy Seuss?

—What do you mean?

—Well, with all due respect, I saw his tryout, and he's not very good.

—Not very good? Billy Seuss might be the most uncoordinated boy in California. The other kids call him "Polio."

—So then why does everyone want to get him on their team?

—Did you ever see his mother—Connie Seuss?

—No.

—She's a real looker.

When I was growing up, I was a good ballplayer—though not as good as my son is. And certainly not as good as I tell my son I was. But I never had trouble making a team, and I was always a starting player. But now that I think about it, my mother was very pretty back then. Very, very, pretty. Oh, no. Is it possible that I was referred to as "Polio" Zweibel and wasn't aware of it? Well, that's just lovely.


## THE PRESEASON

    —Hello?

    —Where the hell's the rake?

    —Excuse me?

    —You're the new commissioner, right?

    —Right.

    —So where's the goddamn rake?

What rake? And since when did I become commissioner of gardening tools?

    —Who is this?

    —Gary Drummond, manager of the Pirates. Saturday's our first game, and I need that rake because I don't want my pitcher breaking his ankle stepping into that hole on the mound.

    —Gary?

    —Yes.

    —Your game is Saturday?

    —Yes.

    —And today is only Wednesday?

    —Yes.

    —*Six-thirty in the morning* on only Wednesday?

    —That's not the point.

    —Gary?

    —Yes?

    —I can *build* a rake between now and Saturday!

I usually don't raise my voice like that, but I thought it might be a good idea to assert my new authority from the outset. You know—out of respect for the office of the commissioner. Besides,

I knew who Gary Drummond was. A small guy I was fairly confident I could beat up—unless he had a rake.

—Now look, Gary—

—It's that bastard Rappaport.

—*Skip* Rappaport? The manager of the Astros?

—I'll bet you anything he took that rake out of the shed, because he's still pissed I beat the pants off him in court last week.

—Court?

—Yeah, we're both attorneys, and I just know that shyster is trying to get even by breaking my best pitcher's ankle.

A lot of managers in this league are attorneys. During a preseason game, I saw two disputing a call made by an umpire named Jorge. They were brandishing the Little League rule book and citing the bylaws and subsections therein. For all I know, they're still out there arguing, and Jorge, who speaks twelve words of English, is still standing there weeping.

—Now, what the hell are you going to do about this rake business?

—Well, Gary, I'm still sort of new at this commissioner thing, so I'll call Normie Wax and ask him how I should handle this, and then I'll get back to you, okay?

—Call him now.

—But it's only . . .

—I'm telling you, call him now, because he'll be going into surgery in about an hour.

—Oh, my God. What's wrong?

—Nothing's wrong. He's a surgeon.

—Normie Wax is a surgeon?

I had no idea Normie Wax was a cardiovascular surgeon. Or that Gary Drummond and Skip Rappaport were successful corporate attorneys. Or that Home Depot carried so many different kinds of rakes. I was learning a lot.

—Hi, Alan. It's me, Normie. Look, I was checking over the schedule you made for the season, and everything looks fine except for Thursday, May sixth, where you have all eight teams playing on the same field at two-thirty in the morning. Give me a call, will you?

## THE SEASON

My son had trouble sleeping the night before the first game. So did I. He was nervous. So was I, but I didn't let him know it. Anxious feelings have a memory of their own and have an insidious way of returning when someone you love is experiencing them as you once did. But part of the job of being a father on these occasions is to create innocuous small talk during the drive to the field and then sit in a strategic corner of the bleachers, from where your child can feel your presence but not your nerves.

—We've got a problem.

—Can it wait, Normie? My son's pitching.

—Sorry, but this is urgent.

—What's wrong?

—They canceled *The Rutherfords.*

—What's *The Rutherfords*?

—You know, that stupid sitcom about that moronic mountain family that was part of the Tuesday-night lineup.

—Oh, yeah.

—You know the show?

—No.

—Well, it stunk.

—So, why is this a problem?

—Because Howie Heckler, who created *The Rutherfords,* has a son named Owen who plays for the Indians, as does the kid whose dad is the network exec who canceled the show.

—Oh, boy.

—So, the Hecklers are demanding a trade, which is a big problem for the Indians, because Owen's their best player.

—And what about the executive's kid?

—He's almost as bad as *The Rutherfords.*

—So why not trade *him* instead?

—No can do, amigo.

—How come?

—His old man is giving us the money for a new scoreboard.

—Oh.

I'd heard about this new scoreboard. It was electronic and had a picture of the network executive on it.

—You know something? Jamie Oxnard's not bad. Maybe his manager won't mind trading him for Owen Heckler. Any conflict with *Jamie's* dad?

—It's a nonissue, *kemosabe.* His old man's in jail for taking part in the S&L scandal. So right now, my guess is he's more concerned about who's standing behind him in the prison courtyard than what team his son plays for.

—Jesus, Normie . . .

—I'll go check into that trade.

With that crisis out of the way, I turned my attention back to the game. My son's team took an early lead, and I was starting to relax when a man I did not recognize approached me.

—You the major-league commissioner?

—Yes.

—That your boy who just got that double?

—Yeah.

—Seems like a nice kid.

—Thanks, he is.

—You must be real proud.

—I am.

—I'm real proud of my boy, too.

—Uh-huh.

—But he won't be out here today, and you know why?

—Why?

—Because of you, you prick.

—Excuse me?

—He's twelve years old. Loves baseball—eats, sleeps, and breathes the game. But because you and those other geniuses who run this thing didn't deem him worthy to be drafted onto a major-league team, you can't imagine how devastated he is.

—God, I'm sorry, but . . .

—*You're* sorry? My boy's at home crying while these younger kids are playing because I don't kiss the right asses or because my wife's chest isn't as big as Connie Seuss's—and *you're* sorry? Fuck you, Commissioner.

The man's son was named Henry Dwyer, and at the next board meeting, I was told that Henry was not as good a player as his father thought. And since a kid who's drafted into the majors stays with that same team for the rest of his Little League career, the managers prefer drafting younger players whom they can develop over the next few years, as opposed to a twelve-year-old who's in his last eligible season. I felt bad for Henry Dwyer. But as things turned out, his dad was not the only parent with a gripe.

—*Hi, Alan. It's me, Normie. Look, I'm sure it was only a typo, but a lot of the parents are upset because the flier you sent out said this year's yearbook is going to cost fifteen hundred dollars. Give me a call, will you?*

Two weeks later was my wife's birthday, so I took her to our favorite restaurant to celebrate. Upon being seated, I recognized a nearby couple, who asked the waiter if he wouldn't mind moving them to a table that was farther away from ours. They were Little League parents who were still angry at me for not firing the coach they claimed their nonathletic son was allergic to.

—Alan?

—Yes?

—Normie.

—Hi, Normie.

—How you doin', amigo?

—Fine, Normie.

—Good to hear. Real good to hear.

—Normie?

—Yes.

—Is everything okay?

—Super, just super.

—Then, Normie?

—Yeah?

—Why are you calling me at my parents' house?

—Because we have a problem.

—So things aren't "super, just super"?

—No, they're not.

—What's wrong, Normie?

—Everyone hates you.

—They do?

—Yes, they do.

—Why?

—Because they feel you're using your power as commissioner to favor your son's team.

—I am *not.*

—Well, they see it differently. They're pissed about a bunch of stuff.

—Like what, for instance?

—Daylight saving time.

—Daylight saving time?

—Yep.

—Yep? You say yep as if daylight saving time is a normal thing for anyone to be pissed about. What are you saying?

—Look, I got a call from a parent who was incredibly irate because you scheduled your son's first game in daylight saving time against his son's team, who you eventually beat with a rally in the sixth inning but would've lost to if it'd gotten dark an hour earlier when his son's team was ahead.

—And *that's* why the parents hate me?

—That's why this parent does.

—And who is this parent?

—Barry Spass.

—*Dr.* Barry Spass?

—Yes.

—My dentist? So now you're telling me that my dentist hates me?

—Look, maybe your dentist is overreacting, but if you ask me, I think everyone on that team is still upset about your taking such a hard line last month against their shortstop.

—Mario Ventura?

—He was their best player, but now they won't have him for the play-offs against your son's team because you kicked him out of the league.

—Normie, Mario Ventura lived out of our district.

—Boy, was he good.

—Of course, he was good—he was from the Dominican Republic! Everyone in that country is good! But anyway, what choice did I have? They were threatening to revoke our league charter!

—And what about the Lawrence twins?

—The parents are mad about that, too?

—The *twins'* parents are.

—Normie, I drew up the schedule in February. I don't have a crystal ball. How was I supposed to know back then that both Lawrence twins would make the all-star team in June? Or that the first game of the tournament would conflict with their older brother's Bar Mitzvah? I don't even know the Lawrences, let alone when their older brother turns thirteen!

—So, they were replaced by two players from your son's team.

—Look, I'm trying my best to be fair.

—I'm sure you are.

—Hey, wasn't I the one who offered to drive those twins to the game after the reception? So back off, Normie!

—Okay, okay.

—Anything else? Any other news that's going to brighten my day?

—No, just the banquet.

—What banquet?

—The end-of-the-season banquet. The one that all the kids and their parents and the coaches attend.

—What about it?

—Well, it's the commissioner's job to be master of ceremonies . . . Hello? Hello? You still there?

## EPILOGUE

The season is now over. Last night was the banquet. Speeches were made. Trophies were awarded. And, wearing regular clothes instead of their uniforms, the children looked like children. Children who table-hopped from team to team, while we parents pretty much stuck to our own.

Why we behave this way, I don't know. Do we love our kids so much that we're afraid to let them fail? Or are we selfishly using them to make us feel better about ourselves? Maybe that's it. And maybe it's natural. I know that I sit a little taller in those bleachers when my son gets a hit, just as I suspect my parents may be slightly embarrassed when something I've written is publicly panned.

Right now, our son wants to be a ballplayer when he grows up, and despite the long odds, I'm rooting for him. About a week ago, I drove past the Little League field and saw Henry Dwyer practicing with his dad. And even though they both gave me the finger, I hope Henry makes it, too.

As for me, I'm glad I was commissioner. Sure, it made my life miserable and taught me some very unattractive things about our species. But it also allowed me to keep a protective eye on my boy's dream, as well as reunite me with some old feelings and my missing words.

I Saw Your Mother's Ass

*A husband gets into bed at night. His wife speaks first.*

—You okay?
—Not really.
—Want to talk about it?
—Not really.
—Honey, what's wrong?
—Can't say.
—Why?
—It's too weird.
—What's too weird?
—I'd rather not say.
—Now you're scaring me.
—Why?
—Because we've been married a long time and I've never seen you this color before.
—Can't help it.

—Why?

—Can't say.

—Please tell me.

—Fine.

— . . . Well?

—I saw your mother's ass.

—What are you saying?

—That I saw your seventy-seven-year-old mother's seventy-seven-year-old ass.

—How?

—I was on my way to the bathroom, a door was open, and there it was in all its horrifying glory.

—God, she must've been embarrassed.

—No.

—No?

—No.

—Why not?

—Because she didn't see me.

—How's it possible that you walk in on someone in the bathroom and they don't see you?

—Because she wasn't *in* the bathroom.

—But you just said . . .

—I said that I was on my way to the bathroom.

—Oh . . .

—And I passed the gym, innocently looked in, and saw your mother on my stationary bike.

—Naked?

—Like a seventy-seven-year-old jaybird.

—From behind?

—Yes. That's where her ass is. In the back.

—Wow.

—Yeah. Wow.

—I think you'll get over it.

—I'm not so sure about that. In fact, I'm wondering how I can ever look at her again. In fact, I'm wondering if you and I should separate and get back together after she dies.

—You wouldn't be overreacting, would you?

—Trust me, any normal man would be mortified.

—Come on, you've seen her in a bathing suit. I'm sure there were no surprises.

—Not so.

—What do you mean, "not so"?

—I can't talk about it.

—What can't you talk about?

—I can't tell you. Now let me go to sleep, okay?

—Fine.

—Good night.

—Good night.

*He turns off the light for about six seconds, then turns on the light and speaks.*

—Did you know your mother has a tattoo?

—She does?

—Yep.

—Where?

—On her ass.

—She does not.

—I'm telling you . . .

—Oh, please . . .

—If you don't believe me, go downstairs and see for yourself.

—No, thanks.

—You're right—I should be the only one in this bed who's scarred for life.

—She really does?

—Why would I make this up? Why would I possibly want this conversation to go any longer than it already has?

—May I ask what it's a tattoo of?

—You sure you want to know?

—No. But tell me anyway.

—Ready?

—Yeah.

—Hitler.

—Hitler?

—Yep.

—My seventy-seven-year-old mother has a tattoo of Adolf Hitler on her ass?

—That's right. And I must say that the führer looks less than thrilled to be there.

—Hard to blame him . . .

—Yeah, I feel bad for Hitler, too.

—And you're sure that you're not making this up?

—I'm not . . .

—Or mistook, let's say, a mole, for Hitler?

—A mole for Hitler? No. And I didn't mistake cellulite for Goebbels, either. This is a tattoo and it's Hitler, and if you don't believe me, go down and take a look for yourself.

—I think I will.

—Fine.

*She gets out of bed, leaves the bedroom, and returns about a minute later.*

—You're right. It's Hitler.

—Told you.

—Yes, but what you didn't tell me was that every time my mother pedals, Hitler's arm comes up in one of those Third Reich salutes.

—I thought I'd spare you.

—Thanks.

—So, what do we do now?

—What do you mean?

—Well, we've solved the mystery of who the tattoo is. Aren't you at all curious as to why it's there? As to why your seventy-seven-year-old Jewish mother, who's been a registered Democrat since Truman was president, has a picture of the man who thought of the Final Solution on her butt?

—Yeah . . .

—Did she ever date Hitler?

—What?

—You know, they were young, impulsive, had too much to drink one night, took a cab downtown and got tattoos of each other before she realized he wasn't such a great guy.

—That's the scariest thing I've ever heard.

—How so?

—Because according to that scenario, Hitler, who was arguably the worst human being who ever lived, had a tattoo of my mother on *his* butt.

—Well . . .

—You're saying that in all those newsreels when he was giving those speeches and goose-stepping in those parades and invading Poland he may have had a picture of my mother on his ass.

—Anything's possible.

—Jesus, could we please end this conversation?

—I'd love to.

—Fine. Good night.

—Good night, honey.

*They turn off their lights. About a minute later, he speaks.*

—I can't sleep.

—Neither can I.

—I keep thinking about your mother's ass.

—I keep thinking about Hitler's ass.

—And I keep thinking I'll need a new seat for my stationary bike.

# The Kirschenblatt Affair

Before the student of moral philosophy can fully appreciate the case of Jerome and Phoebe Kirschenblatt, it is important for him to understand what is meant by a dilemma. By definition, it is merely a state in which an individual has to make a choice between two practical options. But within the context of a moral situation, the conflict is far more complex and the consequences of the ultimate decision far more profound.

*FOR EXAMPLE:* Joey, age nine, is seated at the dinner table with his parents and his sister, Melody. As the appetizer is being served, Joey's mom politely asks him if he'd please pass the salt. Little Joey, for some reason uncharacteristically rude, replies, "Your time's up, bitch" and throws a cleaver at her thorax. Although Mom somehow escapes injury, Joey knows that Dad is sore at him and means it when he says, "No son of mine will throw a cleaver at the dinner table. Go upstairs to your room!"

*SITUATION:* Hearing his father's angry words, Joey knows he has a problem. He can't go upstairs to his room because he and his family live on the roof.

*ISSUE:* Joey has a moral dilemma. Does he choose not to honor his father and chance violating the fifth commandment? Or does he try to go upstairs—thus breaking the law of gravity? A tough choice indeed—especially for a nine-year-old whose sister's name is Melody. What would you do?

Is there a correct choice in this situation? Rabbi Jeff Abramson of the Jewish Theological Seminary answers, "In most moral situations, I don't think there is a right or a wrong." This sagacious profundity is further upheld by the Reverend Fulton Sheen, who recently told a symposium of moral philosophers, "I think I agree with Jeff." A moral dilemma can present itself in many forms and can be catastrophic to one of the parties who's dependent on the decision. It is then that the student of moral dilemmas must pay closer attention to certain factors that must be considered before making such a decision.

*FOR EXAMPLE:* Mrs. Lynch returns from the grocery to find her home on fire—with both of her children trapped in two adjacent rooms. Entering the house, she realizes that she can save only one of the kids. What should Mrs. Lynch do? On what basis should she make her decision?

1. Should whether or not either of the children finished their homework influence her decision?
2. Suppose one of the children had a winning lottery ticket in his pocket?
3. Do you think that Mrs. Lynch could have saved both children had she put down her groceries?

4. Suppose Mrs. Lynch was seventy-five years old and her children were forty-six-year-old identical twins, both firemen?

It should be noted that while not all moral dilemmas present themselves as life/death situations, most jurists and Talmudic scholars agree that those that do are the funniest. However, there are instances where ethical decisions have to be rendered by legal authorities—the results of which are still subject for debate between the religious and secular communities. Justice Holmes, after months of deliberation, was roundly ridiculed in a clash between the church and the state for his decision that an unruly Amish student could refuse to "button his lip" and not fear reprisal. And most recently, the *Olive* decision (*Green* v. *Black*) offered that if you have a friend who's president of the botanical gardens, it's okay to kill him if he's going away for the weekend and asks you to water his plants.

The Kirschenblatt affair, while not considered unique in the study of ethical analyses, is often cited because of its myriad ramifications and illustrates the dynamics of problem confrontation and sound decision making.

*FOR EXAMPLE:* David H. needs money but has no job. In a moment of sheer desperation, he grabs a toy pistol, enters Kirschenblatt's Bakery, takes a number, and, when it is his turn, brandishes the "weapon" and demands cash. Not knowing that it is a toy pistol, Mr. Kirschenblatt faints, hits his head on the counter, goes into shock, and suffers a concussion, a heart attack, kidney failure, a collapsed lung, a broken spine, diabetes, a ruptured spleen, and gross-motor-skill impairment before finally lapsing into critical condition. Since the weapon was not a real

gun, is David H. guilty of murder? If you were a judge, how would you vote?

A difficult decision for any man on the bench, but perhaps not as agonizing as the one that now confronts Mrs. Kirschenblatt. Realizing that business at the bakery could not possibly cover the mounting medical bills (unless every day miraculously turns into Sunday morning), Mrs. Kirschenblatt decides to convert the study into a bedroom and rent it to a boarder. This seems like a wise idea, as it will both provide income for the household and, should Mr. Kirschenblatt recover, allow him not to feel compelled to spend countless hours alone trying to figure out what a baker should do in a study.

The Kirschenblatts reside in a white, middle-class neighborhood that abides by a gentlemen's agreement not to allow blacks into the community. However, the ad for a boarder that runs in the local paper is answered by a black man. He seems respectable, well spoken, and courteous. Plus, he offers to pay a full year's rent up front, in cash. This proposition would certainly be a boon to the Kirschenblatts, given the financial crisis they are undergoing. So now Mrs. Kirschenblatt has a moral dilemma. She knows that if she were to refuse to rent the room to this black man, it would infuriate the NAACP. But on the other hand, she knows that it would bother her husband and perhaps aggravate his condition if she rented the room to a black man—still at large—who had held up his bakery with a toy pistol. What would you do?

"Practicality," says the Reverend Dr. William Prath, "should dictate the decision made in even the most morally extenuating circumstances." Mrs. Kirschenblatt needs money to help her husband, whom she loves. And to her, this love outweighs her desire for vengeance against the man who was the cause of her troubles. Compassion is indeed a virtue of Mrs. Kirschenblatt. "And besides," she reasons, "if this black man has enough money to live in a well-to-do neighborhood like this, he must be of a better breed than the rest of those people."

So David H. moves in, but while the rent money does ease the financial situation somewhat, it becomes evident that it is not enough. Mr. Kirschenblatt's condition stabilizes enough for him to be taken home. However, intense pain renders him delirious, and he hardly speaks anymore except for an occasional outburst, when he'll moan, "Hi, I'm Gene Rayburn, welcome to *Match Game 79*," and then go back to sleep. But there is one drug that the doctors think might save him. It is a form of radium that Jack Davis, a local druggist, carries. Though it costs him five hundred dollars to buy it from the pharmaceutical lab, Davis sells it for two thousand dollars. Mrs. Kirschenblatt borrows as much money as she can from friends and relatives but is only able to raise a thousand dollars. She tries desperately to convince Jack Davis that the medicine will relieve Mr. Kirschenblatt's torment and that at a thousand dollars Davis would still make a nice profit. But Davis is adamant. "My dear Mrs. Kirschenblatt, I'm a businessman. If I give you a break, then before you know it, every woman with a pain-racked husband will want a similar bargain. I'm sorry. I hope your husband feels better. Really I do. But I have to be strong. I can't give in. It was weakness on my part that made things go sour for Beverly and me. Our marriage might have been saved had I provided her with the strength that she needed from a man. But I was a fool and I hurt her. God, I do regret it. I'm so lonely. Please sleep with me, Mrs. Kirschenblatt, and you can have the medicine for half price."

An affair for money? Adultery? Infidelity? Mrs. Kirschenblatt has a moral dilemma. Of course an extramarital relationship is something that goes totally against her principles—but Mr. Kirschenblatt will need that medicine even more as the pain increases and he can no longer exhale without taking a running start. For the sake of her dear husband, should Mrs. Kirschenblatt break the eighth commandment, a tenet that she holds dear? What would you do?

Mrs. Kirschenblatt decides to sleep with Jack Davis. Not enjoying a second of it. She feigns both affection and ecstasy. She tells Jack that she loves him. That she understands him. And that yes, Momma was right—pharmacists do make the best lovers.

When it is over, Jack closes the drugstore for the evening and escorts Mrs. Kirschenblatt home to show her how to administer the medicine. It is a lovely evening and Mrs. Kirschenblatt begins to ruminate about the vagaries of life. How unpredictable everything is. After fifteen years of faithfulness to one man, she is now walking with a stranger whom she has given herself to, to save the man she loves. But would Mr. Kirschenblatt understand her decision? Would he forgive her? Would he rationalize that it was his well-being that motivated her and ultimately justified her immorality? Yes, he would. It might hurt at first, but in his heart he'd know that her violation was committed only because she loved him—and that the act itself was meaningless in the long run.

This realization comforts Mrs. Kirschenblatt until they return to her home to find her house on fire—with Mr. Kirschenblatt and the black boarder trapped in two adjacent rooms. Entering the house, she realizes that she can save both of them, but only if Jack Davis assists her. She looks beseechingly at the beleaguered druggist, who now has a moral dilemma. Should he risk his life trying to save two people whom he doesn't know or really care about? Or should he ignore the pleas of a woman who, in effect, charged him the outrageous price of a thousand dollars for fifteen minutes of cheap, insincere sex?

Jack Davis grabs the medicine, pushes Mrs. Kirschenblatt into the fire, and goes home. What would you have done?

## Stationery Stores

I believe stationery stores—that's right, stationery stores—are the most romantic places in the world. More so than an empty beach in the morning, a moonlit park at night, or a sunset at, well, at sunset. Mind you, I'm not talking about the big kinds of so-called stationery stores like Staples or Office Depot with their high ceilings, wide aisles, and shopping carts big enough to transport small homes from one zip code to another. I hate those places because they're cold, impersonal, and don't even remotely smell like stationery stores.

Yes, it's an olfactory thing that my receptors respond to—the same way they do to the proper kind of bakeries. But in order for the subtle aromatic mix of composition books, reinforcements, pencil cases, and protractors to effectively evoke sense memory the way old songs do, they must be contained within more intimate confines so their magical scents cannot dissipate. Places that can carry only six compasses, not six hundred. Where pens that cost more than $4.99 are locked inside of a display case, as opposed to living in big bins. And where the smell of blue loose-leaf books is not polluted by the plastic emissions of those im-postors made of fake leather and referred to as binders. It's comparable to the way a baseball game smells at Wrigley Field as opposed to how it smells at one of those huge new stadium complexes. One smells like baseball, the other like an office building.

My favorite stationery store is about a mile from my house. It's a small place that's sandwiched between a Blockbuster and a Circuit City—both of which I also hate. So whenever I'm expe-riencing writer's block, all I have to do is step into that store and I smell third grade. And Mrs. Kasarsky's hair. And the state cap-itals. And the phrase "cursive writing." And my crush on Bar-bara Graber. And how I wrote her name a thousand times on a book cover that said "Green Bay Packers" on it. And how she once needed to borrow a pencil for an arithmetic quiz we were having. And how I tried to get on Barbara's good side by quickly unzipping my pencil holder, pulling out a freshly sharpened #2, and handing it to her before Steven Snipper, who also had a crush on her, could lend her one of his. And how I blew any chance of her liking me back because, in my haste, I accidentally stabbed her in the hand because I forgot that pencils (like scis-sors) should be handed to the other person with the sharp end facing the person doing the handing over. The pencil point broke off in Barbara's palm and remained there for the rest of elemen-tary school, junior high, and high school. A subcutaneous, graphite reminder that I saw close up whenever I asked her out and she held up her hand and shook her head. I tried to apolo-gize. I even wrote her a sonnet once (on really nice stationery) waxing poetic about how Leonardo da Vinci accidentally poked Mona Lisa with a pencil point and that's why her hands were folded in the painting, but Barbara didn't budge. Was it possible that she simply wasn't attracted to me and was using the pencil incident as an excuse to spare my feelings? Possibly so—which made me love her that much more for being so considerate of my fragile emotions.

Today, my three children think I'm insane when I tell them that I can smell my entire life in that little store and that they may very well starve to death should it ever go out of business. But having shopped for stationery only at Staples, and for pastry in large supermarkets, and for shoes in even larger department stores, they can't really be blamed for not relating—though I must confess that I consider it their loss and truly worry that they may not have any nostalgic smells in their futures.

By the way, I recently ran into Barbara Graber. My thirtieth high school reunion. She was there with her husband, Steven Snipper, the guy who didn't stab her with a pencil at the exact moment that I did. And though I am happily married and have a great family, when I saw that pencil point, which is still embedded firmly (and at this juncture I guess it's safe to say permanently) in her palm, I couldn't help but wonder what would've happened had I handed over that pencil with the eraser facing her.

## True Crime: Me on the Streets of L.A.

Writing is rather precarious work, given that the margin of error between what's considered a classic and a folly can be ever so slight. For example, it's a well-known fact that the screenplays for *The Godfather* and *Bubble Boy* used the exact same words but in a different order. Still, I never really knew just how dangerous my chosen profession was until one of my credits recently came back to haunt me.

Back in 1987, I was a co-writer on the film *Dragnet,* which inspired a magazine editor to ask if I'd like to write a piece about True Crime: Streets of L.A.—one of the most popular video games since its release last year.

For those of you unfamiliar with this game, the object is simple. An indescribable hell has been unleashed by ruthless gangs, so it was my job to drive, fight, and shoot my way through 240 miles of Los Angeles streets in an attempt to rid our city of this scourge. And the tour guide is rapper Snoop Dogg, whose presence made perfect sense. The music of this former Crips member would provide the experience with a hard-driving, realistic score in the fight against urban evil.

But here comes the wrinkle. I was asked to imagine what would happen if Sergeant Joe Friday, the stiff, monotoned character from *Dragnet,* had inexplicably found himself in the game—and his partner was no longer Officer Bill Gannon but Snoop D-O-double G.

JOE FRIDAY

9:56 A.M. I'm patrolling the streets of this city. Los Angeles, California. Four thousand one hundred and thirteen square miles of constantly interfacing humanity representing every race, color, creed, and persuasion.

SNOOP DOGG

Who you talkin' to? And why the hell we up at 9:56 A.M.? Ain't no gang activity going on in the morning. Homeboys be sleeping.
*(starts rapping)*
*If you're white or if you're black,*
*This is something to groove to,*
*Made to move to, ensue you, like Snoop do.*

JOE FRIDAY

The fact is, Officer Dogg, "ensue you" is not an expression that exists in the English language. You can't ensue someone. And if you could, trust me, buster, you wouldn't be the one I'd want to ensue me.

SNOOP DOGG

Chill, biatch. You gettin' my doggy underwear in a bunch. Let's just blunt out and
relax. Fo' shizzle?

JOE FRIDAY

Fo' what?

So after I had Timothy (the nine-year-old kid who lives across
the street) come over and hook up the game, I began to play. But
once their ride started, Snoop Dogg and Joe Friday found themselves confronted by a danger far greater than the militarily
armed thugs they were assigned to combat. Specifically, that a
fifty-year-old sedentary writer who barely had the hand-eye co-
ordination to use a Q-tip without incident was now at the controls of the PlayStation.

Backward and forward I sent them. Crashing into a bus. A
FedEx truck. And one of those little vans that transport blind
people. The car then jumped a curb, bent a fire hydrant, pinned
a mailman to the side of the Staples Center, entered the Ahman-
son Theater through a third-floor balcony window, then somehow found its way onto the 10 Freeway after mowing down a
troop of Cub Scouts on a field trip to City Hall.

JOE FRIDAY

10:38 A.M. I just soiled my Friday underwear.

What amazed me the most at this point was that I was now
driving the car upward of 200 mph during rush hour on a freeway that I'd sat in bumper-to-bumper traffic on for an inordinate chunk of my adult life. And because I had a relatively clear

road ahead of me (with the exception, of course, of the occasional sniper), I began to get a feel for the controls and was actually enjoying the ride. La Brea. Robertson. Overland. I leaned back and relaxed as the exits whizzed by me. I would have put the top down had it not been armor that weighed about seven hundred pounds.

JOE FRIDAY

Traffic's light today.

SNOOP DOGG

That's 'cuz this tricked-out pimpmobile just waylaid the whole town.

JOE FRIDAY

This is no pimpmobile, Junior. This is a standard-issue LAPD undercover vehicle with minor modifications to accommodate investigation and pursuit.

SNOOP DOGG

Damn, Friday. You gotta learn to chill. Take some free time and kick it with your boys.

JOE FRIDAY

I chill just fine, hophead, and I spend my free time at church, "kickin' it" with my boy upstairs.

SNOOP DOGG

Yeah, which church you go to?

JOE FRIDAY

All of them.


It was when I got off the freeway to see if my own neighborhood was depicted that I got into trouble. I took the Bundy exit at a brisk 210 mph, flipped over onto the 405, slid upside down to Wilshire Boulevard, and the car didn't right itself until after I leveled what used to be my favorite Japanese restaurant on San Vicente.

Deep into Brentwood the car sped. Past familiar shops. The post office. Whole Foods. And though steering was no longer a problem, slowing down was, and the ride became increasingly painful as the car took flight every time it went over one of the extraordinarily high speed bumps that couldn't have been more than twenty feet apart.


SNOOP DOGG

Damn it, Flattop. What's with all the road humps?


JOE FRIDAY

Customary in a residential neighborhood to reduce vehicle speeds without adversely affecting intersection operations.


SNOOP DOGG

In my neighborhood, we want to slow down traffic, we pop a cap in somebody's butt. Hustlas and Gold Teefas be chill when there's a 187 investigatin'. Ah, shiz-nit. I think I just bit my tongue.

In an attempt to slow down, I pressed a button, which I prayed was a brake. Unfortunately, it was a Gatling gun, which immediately reduced a neighbor's cat to a pile of teeth and fur. Another button separated the president of our Neighborhood Watch from three of his limbs. And in a desperate attempt to avoid plowing into a boy who looked like Timothy, I swerved, shredded two people who looked like Timothy's parents, and spayed what looked like Timothy's collie before the car became airborne and eventually came to rest on what looked like my front lawn.

### JOE FRIDAY

2:23 P.M. Brentwood, California. Home of the elite, and the elite's accountants. System failures and equipment malfunctions have sabotaged our mission with unfortunate ramifications. Collateral damage was unavoidable.

### SNOOP DOGG

Damn, Joe. I'm the first brother they've even seen in these parts since O.J. pulled that stunt, and look what we just did.

### JOE FRIDAY

This is peanuts. You wouldn't believe what we got away with when Willie Williams was still in charge.

### SNOOP DOGG

Friday, you one crazy cop.

JOE FRIDAY
Fo' shizzle, Officer Dogg. Fo' shizzle.

This is why I write. Twenty minutes behind the wheel and I had managed to cause more death and destruction to the City of Angels than the riots and the Northridge earthquake combined. It was just a game you say? Maybe so. But just the same, I know that if I was out on the roads delivering pizzas rather than locked within the confines of my office moving words around, the results wouldn't be much different. So in the end, this assignment served a purpose—aside from calling attention to my general lack of dexterity. It drove home the point that despite the occasional critical backlash, I know that I am meant to write. Trust me, it's safer for all of us.

# Between Cars

SCENE: *Two tollbooths on a deserted parkway exit. The lighting suggests that it is about 4:00 A.M.*

*He (34) is in the right tollbooth. She (31) is in the left booth. Both are dressed in their Port Authority blues: blue pants, blue shirt, blue hat, etc.*

AT RISE: *She is leaning out of her booth—her arm extended and her hand cupped; ready to accept a toll should a vehicle happen to come along. Meanwhile, he is standing at attention with his right hand over his heart.*

HE
*(singing)*
Gave proof through the night
That our flag was still there . . .

*While singing, he leans back into his booth, leans back out, and throws a coin into the "exact change" basket, causing the toll-gate between their two booths to rise with a dinging sound.*

> HE
> *Oh, say does that star-spangled*
> *Banner yet wave . . .*

*Ding, the arm lowers.*

*No response from her.*

*He leans back into the booth, grabs another coin, leans out, and tosses it into the basket:*

> HE
> *O'er the land of the free . . .*

*Ding, the gate rises and falls.*

*Still no response.*

> HE
> *And the home of the brave.*
>         *(imitates a "stadium roar")*
> Play ball!

*He leans back into the booth—this time producing a basket-ball, which he throws into the basket, banking it off the side of her booth—ding. The gate rises and falls as the ball disappears into the change chute of her booth.*

SHE
*(maintaining her posture)*
Could you please stop?


HE
Hey, she talks. You know, for a minute there,
I was worried about you. Thought you
couldn't talk. . . . Hi. I'm Roger. . . . Roger
Schwing. . . . And you are . . . ?


SHE
Trying to do my job.


HE
Trying to do your job.


SHE
And you're ruining my concentration.


HE
You gotta be kidding.


SHE
Why?


HE
Oh, I don't know. Maybe because it's four
o'clock in the morning. Maybe because it's
January and this road leads to the beach. Or
maybe because there hasn't been a car that's
even come close to this place since Labor Day
and you're standing there like the Statue of

Liberty. That's it! That's why I think you
gotta be kidding.

*She relaxes her pose.*

> HE *(cont'd)*
> Come on, what's your name?

> SHE
> . . . Robin.

> HE
> Good name.
> *(obviously lying)*
> My mom's name is Robin. . . . My dad
> too. . . . They were gonna name *me* Robin,
> but people would've gotten confused be-
> tween me and my brother, Robin Jr.

> SHE
> Why are you lying?

> HE
> Because I'm bored to death. Come on, let's
> play Candy Land.

*He produces the game. She repositions herself with her hand out.*

> HE
> Okay then. How about jacks?

*He runs out, bounces a rubber ball, and throws some jacks. He
puts the ball into her outstretched hand.*

SHE

Can't you understand that it's my first day of work and that I don't want to get into any trouble?

HE

With who?

SHE

Our boss?

HE

What boss?

SHE

Don't we have a boss?

HE

I've never seen a boss.

SHE

How's that possible?

HE

Look, I took the civil service test in a room, all by myself. Then I got that letter saying that I passed the test and that I should come to this tollbooth for the midnight-to-nine shift. So, I get here at quarter to twelve, there's no one here, I stay until nine while nothing that even resembles a car *or* a human being comes by, then I go home.

SHE

How long have you been doing this?


HE

Seven weeks.


SHE

So what do you do every night to keep from going crazy?


HE

I count the different states on all of the differ-ent license plates on all of the different cars that come through here! It's great! Did you ever play that game when you were a kid? It's great fun! Educational, too.


SHE

But you said that no cars have come here since Labor Day.


HE

Absolutely. Which is why no car with *any* kind of license plate will get in our way if we . . .


*He produces two badminton rackets and a net, which he attaches to the booths.*


HE *(cont'd)*

. . . attach the net to both of our booths, and play a few games of . . .

SHE

No!!!

*She realizes she was too emphatic.*

SHE *(cont'd)*

I mean, "No, thank you."

HE

Okay.

SHE

Nothing personal. It's just that . . .

HE

I understand.

SHE

You do?

HE

*(nodding)*

I'm coming on too strong, right?

SHE

*(smiling)*

No, it's just that . . .

HE

It's just that I was coming on too strong.
Well, we'll fix that.

*He goes back into his booth.*

*A beat.*

*The phone rings in her booth. After three rings, she answers it.*

> SHE
> *(into phone)*

Hello?

> HE
> *(into phone)*

Hello, Robin?

> SHE
> *(into phone)*

Yes?

> HE
> *(into phone)*

Hello, Robin, this is Roger. . . . Roger Schwing . . . from next door.

> SHE
> *(into phone)*

Hello, Roger.

> HE
> *(into phone)*

Look, Robin—I realize that this is real short notice and everything, but I was wondering if you'd like to get together tonight.

SHE
*(into phone)*

Well . . .

HE
*(into phone)*

Like I said, I know this is the last minute and
if you do have plans, I'll understand, but . . .

SHE
*(into phone)*

Well, as a matter of fact, I did have some
other things . . .

*He leans out of his booth and screams across to her.*

HE

What other things?
*(into phone, modulated)*
Hello, Robin?

SHE
*(into phone)*

Yes?

HE
*(into phone)*

It's Roger, from next door.

SHE
*(into phone)*

Hello, Roger.

HE
*(into phone)*
Would you like to go out tonight?


SHE
*(into phone)*
. . . Okay.


HE
*(into phone)*
Four-thirty okay with you?


SHE
*(looking at her watch)*
Yeah, okay.


HE
See you then.


*She thinks about getting ready for the date and pulls down the shade.*

*Inside his booth, he begins to get ready for his date. He pulls down a revolving rack and turns it on. It circles around him in the booth, revealing all the items he will need for his date, including toiletries and clothing.*

*As he changes his shirt and anoints himself with the appropriate lotions, brushes his teeth, and ultimately dries his hair by dint of a hair dryer that he plugs in to a socket just below the*

*green light on his booth, he covers all these moves by singing*
*original lyrics to the tune of "If You Knew Susie," making up*
*the words as he goes.*

HE
*(singing)*
*If you knew Robin, like I know Robin,*
*Oh, oh, she collects tolls,*
*She has very short hair,*
*But what do I care?*
*Oh, Oh, I sure hope she bowls . . .*

*I've been out here so long,*
*That even if she, she's hes-it-tant,*
*I am sure that whatever we do*
*Will still be quite pleas-it-tant.*
*If you knew Robin, like I know Robin*
*Oh, oh, I hope it don't rain.*

*On the word* rain *he picks out an umbrella, a box of candy,*
*and a bottle of wine from the revolving rack. He puts them all*
*under his arm and exits his tollbooth, humming and sashaying*
*across to her booth.*

*At her booth, he preens himself one last time, then knocks on*
*her door.*

SHE
*(from inside)*
Who's there?

> HE
>
> It's Roger. . . . Roger Schwing . . . from next door.

> SHE
>
> I'll be right out.

> HE
>
> Take your time.

*He stands there humming "You Can't Hurry Love."*

*A beat.*

*Still humming, he walks to the abutment in front of her booth, bends over, picks a few plastic flowers from it, and walks back to her door with a little bouquet.*

*A beat.*

*He's growing impatient, shifting his weight from one foot to the other and speeding up the tempo of "You Can't Hurry Love."*

> HE
>
> How are you doing in there? Almost ready?

> SHE
>
> Almost.

> HE
>
> Take your time.
>               *(Sotto)*
> "Almost" ready?

*He sings "You Can't Hurry Love" at an accelerated pace, building to an incredible degree of frustration and impatience.*

> HE
> *(under his breath)*
> Where the hell . . . ?

*A beat.*

> HE *(cont'd)*
> *(under his breath)*
> Where the hell . . . ?

*He jumps.*

> HE *(cont'd)*
> Where the hell? Where the hell? Where the hell?

*The door to her booth opens; she comes out, sees him, and watches politely.*

> HE *(cont'd)*
> Where the hell? Where the hell? Where the hell? Where the . . .

*He registers her presence.*

> HE
> Hello, Robin.

> SHE
> Sorry to keep you waiting.

> HE

These are for you.

*He hands her the wine, the chocolates, and the plastic flowers.*

> SHE

You shouldn't have. Thank you.

*A truck passes overhead. She extends her hand—as if to take in a toll—and follows the truck's route with it. He follows her move as she recovers.*

> SHE

Now, what do we do?

> HE

Anything we want. Hey, we're young. We have our health. Want to dance?

> SHE

What?

> HE

Hey, it's Friday night. Date night. Let's go dancing.

*He runs back to his booth, where we hear him rummaging.*

> SHE

Dancing?

*He inserts a CD in a compact-disc player.*

> HE
>
> Dancing.

*He leaves the booth and dances toward her.*

*We hear conga music coming from his booth.*

> HE *(cont'd)*
>
> Conga dancing—let's form a line.

*He puts her hands on his waist and begins to dance.*

> SHE
>
> No!

*He stops.*

> SHE *(cont'd)*
>
> I mean, "No thank you."

*He turns around, grabbing her waist.*

> HE
>
> Would you like to be in the front? Is that the
> problem? Because if it is, I'll gladly let
> you. . . .

> SHE
>
> No, I don't like to conga.

> HE
>
> You don't like to conga?

SHE

Don't get me wrong, this is not to be taken as
a cultural slur on whichever culture in fact
gave us the conga, or to even imply that I
don't fully appreciate the joy that that dance
has brought to our culture when danced at
weddings and Bar Mitzvahs.... It's just
that ...

HE

It's just that *you* don't like to conga.

*She sheepishly nods.*

HE *(cont'd)*

Hey, don't get so down on yourself. A lot of
people don't like to conga.

*He finds another CD, inserts it, and runs back out.*

HE *(cont'd)*

But everyone *loves* the limbo.

*We hear recording of Chubby Checker singing "Limbo Rock."*

*He bows at the waist, does some limbo moves as he travels
around and behind the booths, then leans backward at the waist
as he attempts to limbo under the "exact change" tollgate.*

HE *(cont'd)*

This is fun.

*He sings with Chubby as he dances and limbos. At one point
it's obvious that his stomach is going to hit the "pole." So, in
the limbo position, he reaches into his pocket, grabs a coin, and
throws it into the exact-change basket. The gate goes up, and
he limbos the rest of the way.*

HE

Nothing to it. Your turn.

*She turns away from him. He grabs her from behind; she falls rigidly flat in his arms, yet he tries delicately to push and pull her as if she were a toy, toward the gate. Just when her chest is about to hit the gate, he becomes concerned.*

HE *(cont'd)*

Uh-oh . . . I don't have an extra quarter.

*(fumbles for it)*

Do you have one?

SHE

In my booth.

HE

Oh . . .

*He now pulls her rigid body out from under the gate and stands her in an upright position.*

HE *(cont'd)*

I'll go get it.

SHE

Please don't.

HE

Why not?

SHE

Look, I think I might've made a mistake accepting this date.

                    HE
               *(to himself)*
I've done it again, I took a person and pushed
them a little too far. . . .


                    SHE
It has nothing to do with you. It's just that
I'm not into this right now.


                    HE
Sure.


                    SHE
I'm sorry.


*She turns to go back to her booth.*


                    HE
Is there someone else?


*She stops, nods, and cries.*


                    SHE
Yes. I mean, there was.


                    HE
Is he dead?


                    SHE
No.

> HE
>
> Does he collect tolls?

> SHE
>
> No.

*She turns toward him and blows her nose.*

> SHE *(cont'd)*
>
> He's a chiropodist . . . a foot doctor . . .

*He nods to indicate that he knows what a chiropodist is.*

> HE
>
> I had a bunion once. I could barely put on my shoe. . . .

> SHE
>
> That's why I took this job. To take my mind off things. To throw myself into the work.

*He looks around at the vast nothingness and inactivity that surrounds them.*

> SHE *(cont'd)*
>
> You know what I mean?

> HE
>
> I sure do. And with all due respect, I think I know exactly what you need to help you feel comfortable enough to tell me, a total stranger, your innermost secrets about what went wrong with you and the chiropodist.

> SHE

What's that?

> HE

Wine.

> SHE

Wine?

> HE

Give me a second.

*He runs to his booth, enters, and emerges with two chairs, a folding table, a bottle of wine, and a corkscrew.*

*He quickly sets up the table and chairs.*

> HE

Are you hungry?

> SHE

Not really.

> HE

You sure? Because I'd be more than happy to run over to the beach, drill a hole in the ice, sit there, catch a fish, bring it back here, clean it, and then . . .
> *(indicates his booth)*
cook it in my microwave.

> SHE

No, that's okay.

*They sit. He uncorks the bottle and pours the wine.*

HE

So tell me what happened between you and the chiropodist.

SHE

I screwed up.

HE

You did?

SHE

Real bad.

HE

How?

SHE

I really hated to hurt him.

HE

I understand. But you still haven't told me how you screwed up.

SHE

I don't know . . .

HE

I mean, were you dishonest? Did you deceive him? Did you cheat on him and have safe sex with someone else but then when he asked where you learned all these new moves you insisted that you two have been doing those things all along and accused him of having amnesia but when he said, "I don't have amnesia, Robin," you said that your name was Barbara, so you dropped him like a hot potato and now he's being kept in a special room until the doctors finish their tests but they say they're going to have to take his driver's license away from him no matter what and it's all because of *you*? Did you? Did you? Did you?

SHE
*(smiling)*

No.

HE
You were faithful to him and your feelings?

SHE
Yes.

HE
So? How did you screw up?

SHE
By placing too many unrealistic demands on the relationship. You see, I still have this fairy-tale idea of what romance is supposed

to be. So it always starts off great, but when reality sets in, I get disappointed.

                          HE

I understand.

                          SHE

Sort of makes me never want to fall in love again, because I know I'm just going to end up getting hurt.

                          HE

Well, I don't agree with that.

                          SHE

You don't?

                          HE

No—that's like saying you're not going to get a dog because it's going to die someday. Why deny yourself all that love and all that fun just because you're eventually going to have to say good-bye? The trick with love is to seize the moment it hits you and try to make it last as long as you can, knowing that there are no guarantees.

                          SHE

Hey, that's smart.

                          HE

What's smart?

SHE

What you just said. That whole dead-dog thing.

HE

It is?

SHE

Sure it is.

HE

Wow.

SHE

You didn't know it was smart?

HE

I never said those words before. They made sense when I thought them, but you never know exactly how brilliant thoughts are going to sound until you say them.

SHE

How long have you had these brilliant thoughts?

HE

About seven weeks now.

SHE

Ever since you started working here?

HE

Actually, it's ever since my dad passed away.

SHE

When was that?

HE

About eight weeks now.

SHE

Oh, I'm so sorry. You were close?

HE

Very close. We worked together. He had a factory that he and I ran.

SHE

What kind of factory?

HE

Combs. We made combs.

SHE

Combs? You mean hair combs? Those kind of combs?

HE

Yeah, combs. We made combs. Combs don't grow. They're made. And that's what we did. We made those combs.

SHE

Sounds like your business was very important to you.

HE

Yeah, it was. It was the only business I ever
knew. It was always just assumed that it
would someday be my business, and that was
fine with me—until the day after my father's
funeral. I went to work and looked around at
what was supposed to be my future, and you
know all I saw?

SHE

What?

HE

Combs.

SHE

Combs.

HE

All I saw was plastic teeth and those pocket
holders, which we also made. You see, my
dad was the king of combs, and I was the
prince who was supposed to assume his
rightful place on the comb throne. But now,
with the king gone, there I was, questioning
what I really wanted to be when I grew up.

That's why I took this job, to see what my
next move should be, and when the opportunity presented itself, I'd seize the moment
and become my own kind of king.

SHE

I'm sure you will.

HE

Thanks. And don't worry, your savior will
come.

SHE

My Sir Lancelot?

HE

Sure.

SHE

My knight in shining armor who will slay the
dragon?

HE

If that's what you want him to do.

SHE

And then sweep me off my feet and we'll live
happily ever after in Camelot?

HE

Camelot?

SHE

Camelot.


HE

Then Camelot it shall be.


*He runs to the booth and turns on the CD player.*

*We hear the overture to* Camelot.

*He appears, smiles, and waves, then disappears.*

*A plastic, uninflated dragon comes flying out of the booth and lands between the two booths. It inflates next to her.*

*He emerges, wearing a breastplate and helmet and wielding a sword, just in time to sing at the appropriate musical moment.*


HE

*(singing)*

*Camelot! Camelot!*


*He strides out of the booth toward the dragon.*

*The music continues throughout.*

*His moves are choreographed as such that he approaches her as she cowers, gestures that she needn't be afraid, approaches the dragon, brings his sword back, and keeps hitting the dragon until it eventually deflates.*

*He approaches her, victorious. She now sees him as her noble, heroic knight.*

*He flings down his sword, helmet, and cape. She throws off her coat, revealing a taffeta prom dress.*

*They come together in front of the tollbooths and bow and curtsey respectively, as the tollbooths are transformed into the towers and turrets of Camelot. They start to dance—in between and around the tollbooths—gracefully and romantically to the music.*

*Toward the end of the overture, they dance toward the tollbooth arm, which magically rises; they dance through and stop to sing.*

> HE AND SHE
> *(singing)*
> *. . . for one brief shining moment,*
> *that was known as Cam-e-lot.*

*They almost kiss, as the overture segues into "If Ever I Would Leave You."*

*He walks her back to her booth, where they stop awkwardly, looking tentatively at each other.*

> SHE
> I had a real nice time.

> HE
> Me too.

*A beat.*

                    HE
        Good night.

                    SHE
        Good night.

*He turns and walks slowly toward his booth.*

                    SHE
        Hey, Lancelot!

*He stops walking.*

                    HE
        Yeah?

*He turns to her.*

                    SHE
        What do you say we seize the moment?

*She gestures toward the inside of her booth.*

                    HE
        Okay.

*He runs a few steps toward her, then turns on his heels, rushes to his booth, enters, and rushes out carrying two pillows and a blanket under his arm.*

*He runs about halfway to her booth, again skids to a halt, turns on his heels, rushes back, flips a switch that changes the light over the booths from green to red, runs out, and goes straight into her booth, the door slamming behind him.*

MUSIC

LIGHTS SLOWLY FADE OUT.

## ACKNOWLEDGMENTS

Writing is a solitary act. But making writing my livelihood was a group effort—one that provided me with encouragement, inspiration, and opportunity.

For these invaluable gifts, my gratitude starts with my parents, who at times during an uncertain beginning had more faith in me than I had in myself.

From there, a list forms. It includes those who gave me a chance as well as those who extended a hand when I stumbled along the way. People like Morty Gunty, David Jonas, Lorne Michaels, Gilda Radner, Buck Henry, Herb Sargent, Arnie Kogen, Bernie Brillstein, Don Zakarin, Larry David, Billy Crystal, Rob Reiner, Peter Gethers, Bruce Tracy, Alan Gasmer, Martin Short, Mel Berger, Alison Grambs, and Drew Simon. I've been real lucky. And I thank them all for that luck.

An original *Saturday Night Live* writer, ALAN ZWEIBEL has won multiple Emmy, Writers Guild of America, and TV Critics awards for his work in television, which also includes *It's Garry Shandling's Show* (which he co-created and executive-produced), *Monk,* and *Curb Your Enthusiasm.* In films, he co-wrote the screenplays for *Dragnet, North,* and *The Story of Us.* In addition, he wrote the popular children's book *Our Tree Named Steve* and the 2006 Thurber Prize–winning novel, *The Other Shulman.* His humor has appeared in such diverse publications as *Esquire, The Atlantic Monthly,* and *MAD* magazine, as well as on the *New York Times* op-ed page, and has been reprinted in numerous anthologies around the world. Alan's theatrical contributions include the play *Bunny Bunny: Gilda Radner—A Sort of Romantic Comedy,* which he adapted from his bestselling book. He also collaborated with Billy Crystal on the Tony Award–winning play *700 Sundays,* and with Martin

Short on the Broadway hit *Fame Becomes Me*. A frequent guest on late-night talk shows such as *Late Show with David Letterman*, Alan tours the country doing speaking engagements and performing his own one-man show, which he modestly calls *The History of Me*. But the production that Alan is most proud of is the family that he and wife, Robin, have created with their children, Adam, Lindsay, and Sari, and Adam's wife, Cori.

www.alanzweibel.com

## ABOUT THE TYPE

This book was set in Sabon, a typeface designed by the well-known German typographer Jan Tschichold (1902–74). Sabon's design is based upon the original letter forms of Claude Garamond and was created specifically to be used for three sources: foundry type for hand composition, Linotype, and Monotype. Tschichold named his typeface for the famous Frankfurt typefounder Jacques Sabon, who died in 1580.